# In My Cocoon

*Reyna Noriega*

Also by Reyna Noriega

Prose and Cons, 2017
In Bloom, 2019

# In My Cocoon

by Reyna Noriega

Reyna Noriega

Copyright © Reyna Noriega Studios LLC.
All rights reserved.
© 2021

Cover by Reyna Noriega

Independently published by
Reyna Noriega and Reyna Noriega Studios LLC
www.reynanoriega.com

ISBN: 9798498071770

In My Cocoon

For you,
It's always for you and for us who live and endure and grow. I'm proud of you for making it through. I hope this year you get your wings.

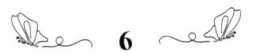

Reyna Noriega

In My Cocoon

## Acknowledgements

I wake everyday amazed at what has transpired in my life, what I have lived through and grown through, and all the opportunities I have been afforded that allowed me to find myself. I feel so grateful for them all, no matter how painful or uncomfortable, for what I have now is peace. The kind of peace that can only come from knowing one's self intimately. To everyone that has read, shared, or gifted my work, know that I am so grateful. You make it possible for me to fulfill my purpose, to continue to enlighten others to how precious their individual journeys are and what each individual lesson can mean.

These books are meant to start conversations both within and amongst your loved ones in safe spaces. Keep doing that, keep healing and sharing and doing the work.

Thank you to everyone that has been a catalyst to my growth, I have forged friendships that have made all the difference. I have loved, been loved, and been left. That has molded me in ways I can only begin to see at the current moment. To my friends that prepared me so selflessly for my big move, hosting me and my last book tour in their cities, connecting me with their resources, and sitting with me in conversation, I owe the success of *In Bloom* to you.

I am the true definition of "it takes a village" and my village has watered me. I am the sum of all my parts and all those that have poured into me. Starting at birth with my parents and family, and evolving into the friendships and partnerships that have blessed my experiences here on earth. This is the part of the journey people often overlook or ignore. The less interesting part of the journey, I guess. We focus on ones talent or the results and forget that talent exists in all of us, power exists in all of us, but some of us never know the beauty of being loved and supported properly so that it may be fully expressed. That is my wish for you. That you get to experience love up close; sisterhood, friendship, true support. I hope

In My Cocoon

that if you don't feel you have that, you learn to be that for someone else. We lose nothing by pouring more love into the world.

When I was at my lowest in 2020, the love I received from my parents, my friends, and my community gave me the strength to continue doing the work so that I could share this with you.

Sandra Noriega, Rey Noriega, Anna Cecilia, Marivette Navarette, Mariela Ramirez, Adrienne Kane, Emmy Vargas, Raquel Flores, Christina Bonnier, Tierra Williams, Ashley Lagares, Ericka Leigh, Amanda Germain, Blake Newton, Amor Capdevilla, DyAnna Moreno, Jeffrey Andre Warner, Roy Handy, Akeeme Hogg, Jasmin Dunn, Jocelynn Ricard, Shantal Rose, Arshayla Robinson, A'Kala Chaires, Nicholas Figaro,

and so many more.

# Contents

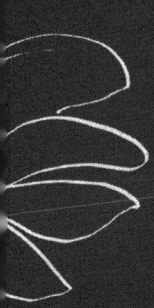

Stage I
19

Stage II
77

Stage III
141

Stage IV
223

Stage V
303

Reyna Noriega

In My Cocoon

## Introduction

I wonder if the caterpillar knows, as it inches along blissfully munching on the leaves, I wonder if it knows that there is more, this is not all there is or will ever be. This is only the beginning. I wonder if the caterpillar knows as it starts to expand and slow, that this is a good thing, for new beginnings are coming. I wonder if it curses the changes happening to its body, comparing itself to its past versions or other caterpillars nearby.

I wonder if the caterpillar knows it will one day be a coveted butterfly and its wings will hold patterns and colors like no other. The appetite grows, unexplainable changes are happening, yet it charges on into the unknown.

I wonder if you know, you are the caterpillar. Soon you too will morph and become a version of you like no version before. All that you've learned and endured is inside you, marinating, waiting for you to mingle with them in isolation, in solitude, in your cocoon.

Every now and then we are forced to pause.
Life events we could not have planned for arise and our world must come to a halt to deal with the repercussions.
A breakup to heal from.
A death to grieve.
A career change to navigate.

We're forced to navigate this while the whole world keeps moving and if we need, there are ample distractions. There are tasks we can get lost in, and friends we can call on. But what happens when the whole world stops and all of the noise you were able to distract yourself with disappears? It's just you, in a room with your loud, loud thoughts and there is only one way to quiet them— Face them.

## In My Cocoon

Take a closer look at the flower that has just bloomed. In the leaves there are holes where the caterpillars have feasted.

And now it rests, curled up in a ball of introspection ready to become the butterfly. Keep feeding on the leaves. Take in all the nourishment you can. This transformation, this metamorphosis, will take all that you have and you'll have to sacrifice all that you are for all you can become.

Holding up the mirror shards, facing your reflection, it will cut and you will bleed. Face it anyway.

I hope seeing what lies beneath my own scars that are nearly healed will encourage you to love your truth. Bask in it. This journey is your own, only you can walk the path. Your highest self is waiting on you to choose them. Your younger self is holding out their hand. Together you are an army. Your peace is the ultimate prize. You have all the strength and all the smarts you will ever need are already inside.

Reyna Noriega

This is the story of a year in isolation. A year of falling into old habits, confronting them, rising above it all. As messy as it was, I don't regret a thing for where it lead me was a place of peace, joy, and unending love.

And what should our existence on this floating rock be if not filled with good things?

# In My Cocoon

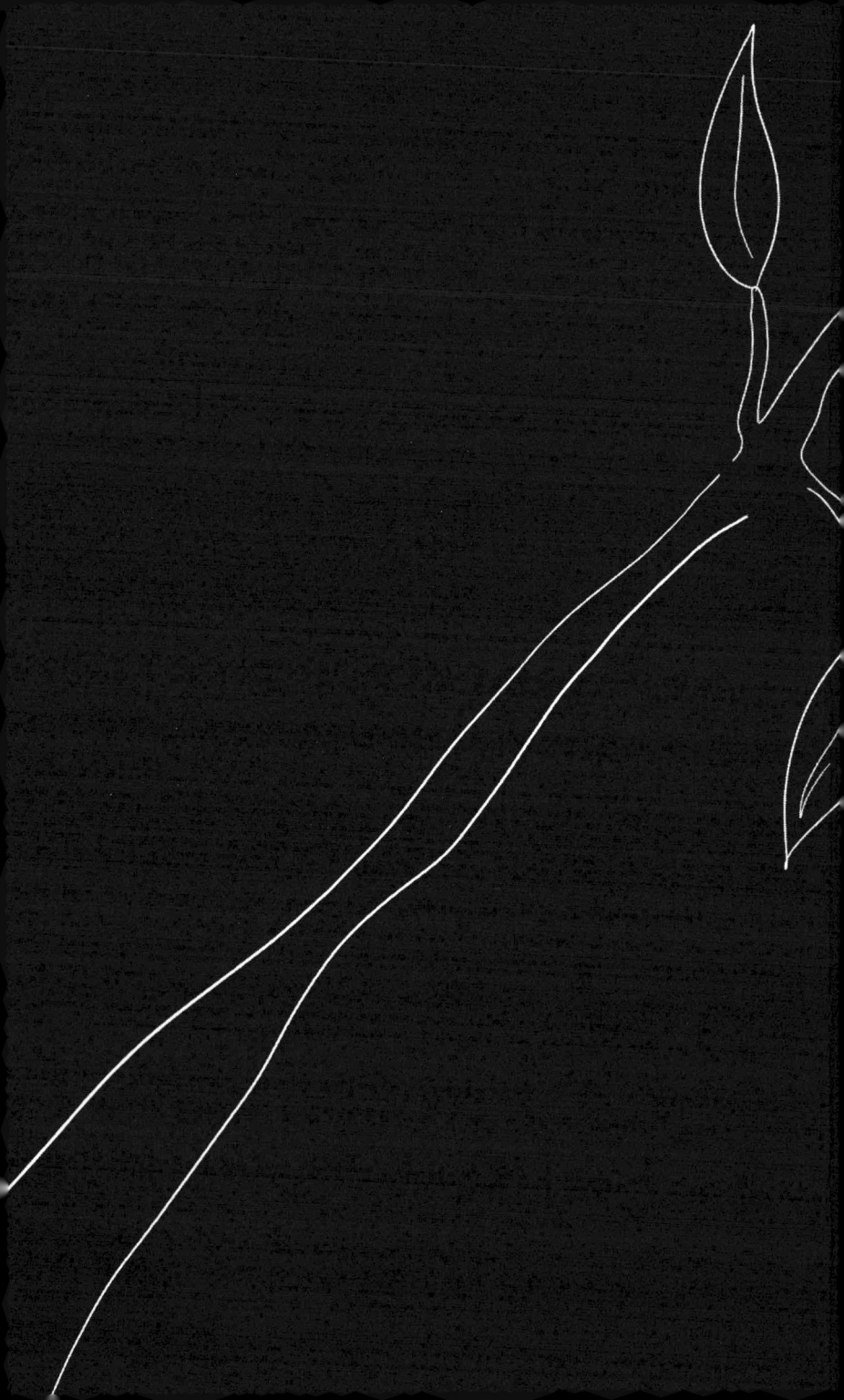

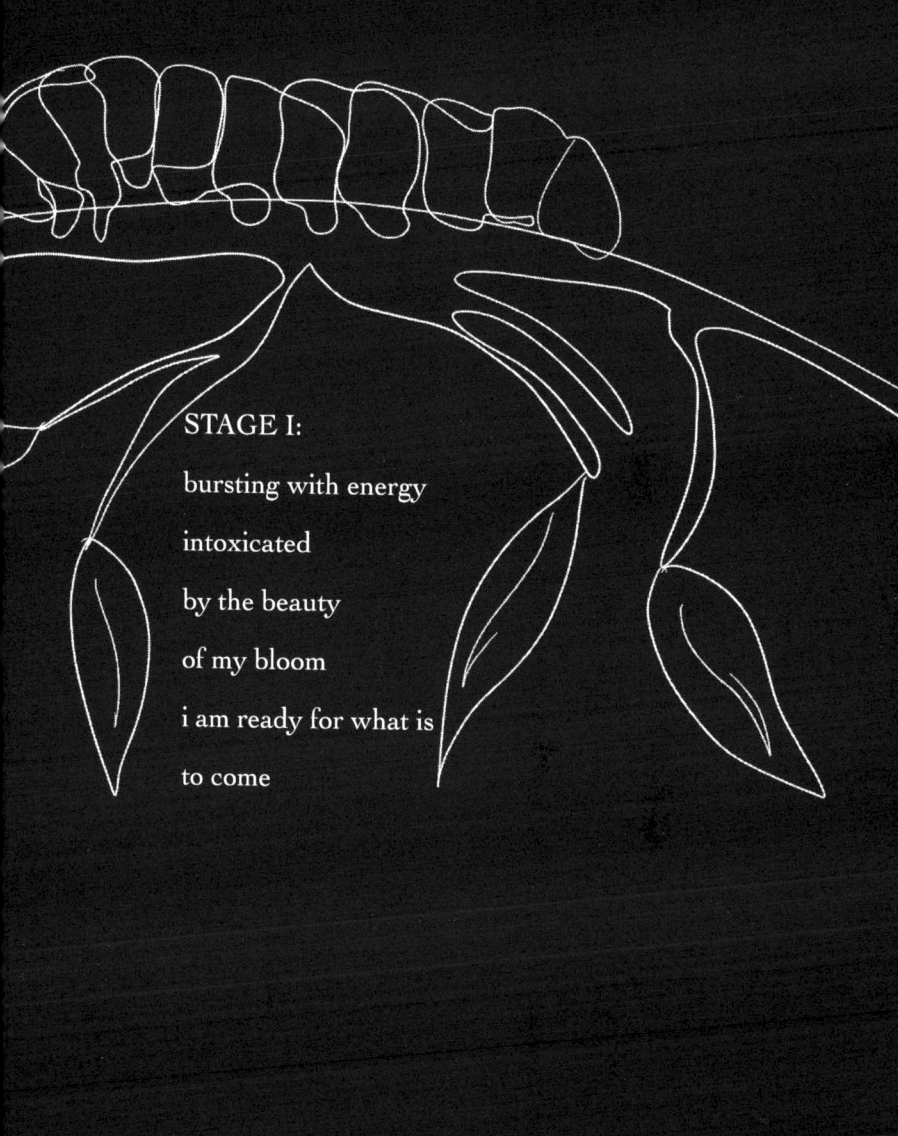

STAGE I:

bursting with energy

intoxicated

by the beauty

of my bloom

i am ready for what is

to come

Reyna Noriega

## In My Cocoon

**3**
no longer an amateur
or a sophomore
mistakes will be
less and less forgivable
each time
but here is book three
i'll never be perfect
but i'm not a newbie either
so i feel naked again
knowing that as more eyes are drawn to me
they may not understand
they may not like my work
and in these moments
i'll have to get over myself
and remember why i share

## Again

i learned so much
now i am understanding so much more
so much deeper i must still go
so i once again prepare
for a journey

In My Cocoon

## **The Secret**

it feels nice
walking around with this secret
like wearing naughty underwear
we make plans
and we joke
so carelessly
and all i can think is
if you only knew
if they only knew —

i'm leaving

Reyna Noriega

## I Won't

i won't tell him
or will i?
i won't tell him i'm going
because i'm not going
for him
this is a dream
i've been alluded by
since i was a kid

but if not for him
and i have nothing to hide
why haven't i told him yet?
is it only pride?

In My Cocoon

## The Knowing

how do i know
it's the right time
how do i know
it's the right move?

because i know what it feels like
to run
to be running away
from self
from growth

i let myself fully bloom here
i let myself outgrow my surroundings
mastered everything this place threw at me
and now i know it's time for a bigger pot

the land of commodity
taught me business
and ambition

and now the land of romance
will mold my work in new ways

## Barcelona

I am embarking on a new journey and that will unlock my dreams. The excitement fills me up. As I dreamed and I planned. I kept this to myself which makes it all the more precious. I will travel to Europe, with only a bag and my best pal Pepper. I will leave behind the rush and the greed and find a new romance between my brush and I. I will walk where the greats walked. I will learn their languages, study where they studied. It will make all the difference.

Of course I will miss my city. I will miss my family and my friends, but no one ever became great without sacrifice and I can think of much worse sacrifices than Barcelona.

*Barcelona*

Choosing her came down to a guess. In meditation I saw a place near the water. Classic architecture, classic look with big city energy. Beyond the coffee shop I sat at, there was so much green. I wonder if I will find that very spot my mind fabricated.

*Barcelona*

She rolls off my tongue. I feel intoxicated.
High from the promises of newness, alluded by wonder and hope.

This will be a refresh, or a rebirth.

I am ready.

## If You're Wondering

If you're wondering if it's time to leave everything behind and start new, I'd say keep wondering.

Ask yourself the important questions —

Do I need change, or do I need to change? Are the people here the problem, or are they lessons? Mirrors carrying the ability to make me elevate if I let them, if I listen.

When you have absorbed all that experience and all of those lessons, when you feel your roots multiplying and tangling in the pot...

Leave.

Start over.

Start new.

In My Cocoon

## Denial

i don't blame them for assuming
i'd move for you
in fact i asked myself that question
many many times
looked in the mirror
long and hard
and asked myself *'what are you expecting?'*
the truth was
this need to travel
to explore the birthplaces of dreams
existed long before you
and because the universe knew
i would trust love long before
i could trust her whispers
she had you usher me
give me just the lightest taste
awaken more dreams
that would later pull me back
but this is my destiny
i have no choice
you and i …
we have a choice

Reyna Noriega

## Few Things

few things offer relief
in this world
where our demons chase us
on turbo speed
one i've found
is to remember
how small we are
in comparison
to our current space
and time
history
the galaxy

travel
remind yourself that a new you
is right across an imaginary border
remind yourself of the vastness of this earth
compare it to your problems

i hope that helps

In My Cocoon

it could be anyone
but i hope it's you.

*-hopeful*

Reyna Noriega

## Plant Parallels

we can learn a lot from plants

if you speak life into it
water it
nourish its soil
it lives

if you want it to do more than live
if you want it to thrive
grow
you must listen
give it what it needs

a bigger pot perhaps

i'm listening to the murmurs of my own heart,
that is what i've decided

i need a new pot for my roots to spread
to grow larger leaves
to stand even taller

In My Cocoon

## Embrace Change

embrace change
change is coming
change is good
what is it about me
that i can feel it coming
my body starts to feel fatigued
as if i were with child
i guess i am pregnant
i will birth something great
i will create something new

Reyna Noriega

## On Body Image

a hand trails up my back
rests along my shoulders
with two light taps
it almost whispers
*too tense*
i roll my shoulders
let them fall
it trails along my body
not judging
not surveying
but appreciating

*this is soft*
*this moves*
*this keeps you mobile*
i agree

my eyes are closed
but it's calling on me to look
look in the mirror
it's me —
i see me
this is my body
the only one i've got

## In My Cocoon

*love her*
i love her
so much i've missed
while trying to change her
i am content

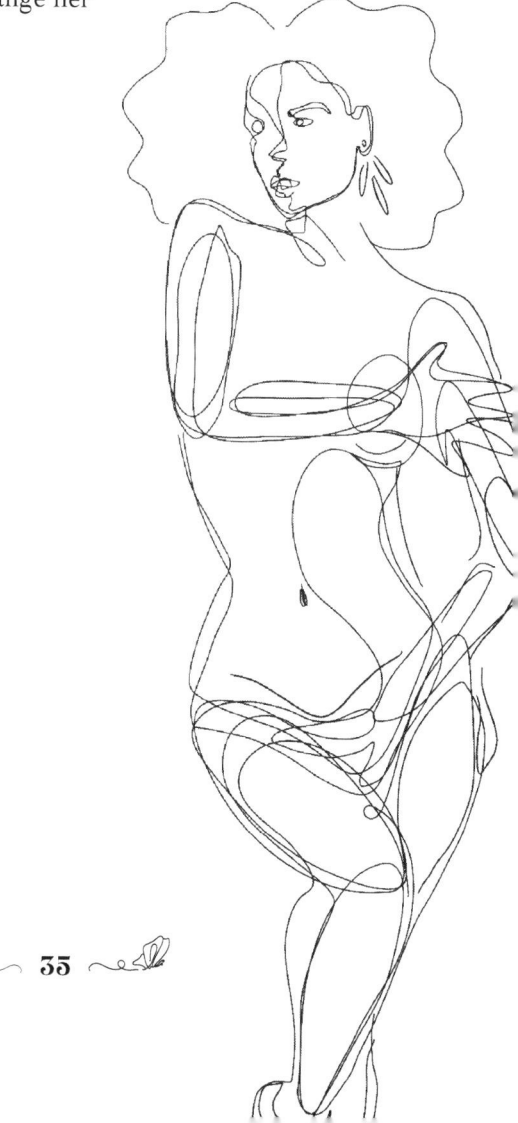

Reyna Noriega

just about anything will grow if you give it time, patience, positive energy, and proper nourishment.

In My Cocoon

## Home

home isn't *anywhere*
home is everywhere

home is you
home is the adventure
home is the people

Reyna Noriega

## Every Time

every time we fight
i go quiet for longer
i hold more in
time and time again
you've proven to be deaf to my needs
your own pride outweighs everything
im tired
i'm defeated
i've been able to change so many hearts
but not yours

i hate crying
it's been so long since i've cried
but you know how to extract the pain
the insecurities

i keep trying to find reasons to forgive you
i keep thinking the next time will be different
it never is
not for long at least

when did our languages get so different
i don't know
but i'm sad

## In My Cocoon

on the eve of my most exciting transition

i still find the silver lining.
maybe i'm meant to go at it alone
but i didn't want to do that
i don't

but if i have to i can
i will

my first best friend.
my maker.
my worst goodbye yet.

Reyna Noriega

## Shrinkage

striving for peace and love
but this is real pain
real disappointment

enlightened and serving a higher purpose
but i have a stress headache

from crying
i tried to be
the bigger person
but you made me feel small
so small

do you wish to shrink me
you wish i were 7 pounds once again
like i was when you birthed me

easy to control
easy to predict
or maybe…

easy to protect

In My Cocoon

## Mom

you reveal your fears to me
it explains your anger
it doesn't excuse it
but with your confessions i'm reminded
you are only human
you don't have the tools,
the words to express yourself
and so your frustrations fall on my shoulders

it's not fair
it is not excusable
but i understand
so i will love you through it

we make up
because i love you
we make up
because i need you
we make up
because *i am*
because of you

Reyna Noriega

## Delay

even the delays work in my favor
i am not worried
i am not mad
i am preparing more carefully

but i wonder,
when

i can already feel the anxiety looming

In My Cocoon

## I Can't Go

not now
not with all that's happening in the world
but what will i do?
i gave up my apartment
all my belongings sold
or locked away in a dark storage unit
what else can i do besides sit here
in isolation
confronting all my lingering demons

Reyna Noriega

## Postponed

I'll never forget canceling that flight. It seemed like I was getting multiple signs from multiple angles to pause.

Wait.

Be patient.

But my determination would not allow me to.

It started with spending 8 hours at the vet when I only had 2 to spare. Not getting anyone from the airline on the phone to confirm if my dog would be allowed in the cabin due to the volume of calls they were getting with COVID-19 cancellations. My living situation being up in the air. A cancelation on my connecting flight. The hostility in my household. The uncertainty of traveling during a pandemic (that hadn't been declared a pandemic yet). It would have been smart to postpone. It would be the right thing to

## In My Cocoon

do. But I waited until the very last minute. Less than 32 hours before departure.

I still remember canceling that flight. I still remember pressing that button. All of the what if's and possibilities dissolving into a thick pool of loss and regret and drowning me.

Admitting defeat was so so hard. Pausing my dream was even harder. No one knew when this would all be over and the optimism I tried to feel, felt like delusion.

I was supposed to be THERE not here. I was supposed to be there NOW not later. All of my dreams were meant to come true as I unfolded into my new self in this new place.

*Barcelona*

I had dreamt about her so many nights. I could practically smell the air. I could taste the coffee. And now I was meant to just wait? Until when? The not knowing was the worst part. Three months? Six? No clue. No one knows. Twelve months later and your guess is still as good as mine.

## Resistance

resistance once again
i don't want to be here
i don't want to wait
but all the signs are saying i must
what can i do with all this idle time
it just makes me anxious
i guess i'll go back to day dreaming

In My Cocoon

## The Longing

i want to love someone
someone i can long for
like i long for him
like i long for my old home

the love hasn't faded
the burns haven't cooled
they are still so potent

Reyna Noriega

## The Man

the kind of man
to help silently
with no need for applause
but to loudly stand up for
what he believes
he is my loud speaker
not my silencer
my dreams are his own
my elevation his pride
my flame his warmth
he smiles,
a lot
for he knows true joy
and in silence he reflects
because he wants to know more

and i get it now
why i couldn't meet this man
when i hoped and prayed i would
he was baking
marinating
becoming
just like me

# In My Cocoon

*i want tenderness.*

Reyna Noriega

## Just For Fun

a breath of fresh air
a welcome distraction
a temporary adventure
i say yes
i oblige
knowing i'm on limited time

In My Cocoon

## I've Got Time

i decide
i've got time to waste
i've got time to play
why not waste it with someone
i can laugh with
why not play with
someone easy on the eyes
and easy on the spirit
what's the worst that can happen
with a quarantine fling...

## Distracted

and during those
few moments with you
it was almost as if
the world as we knew it
wasn't crashing at our feet

In My Cocoon

## In Over My Head

i couldn't go to Europe
so the universe brought it to me

you speak of sculptures
you could be
the work of Michelangelo

you speak the languages
of the lands i wish to roam

you know art
you love music
you dance salsa under the moon
and the glow gets caught in your hair

something tugs at my heart
i wonder if i am in over my head

Reyna Noriega

## You Hold Me Like

you hold me like
you wish our bodies would melt
and merge
so we would never again part

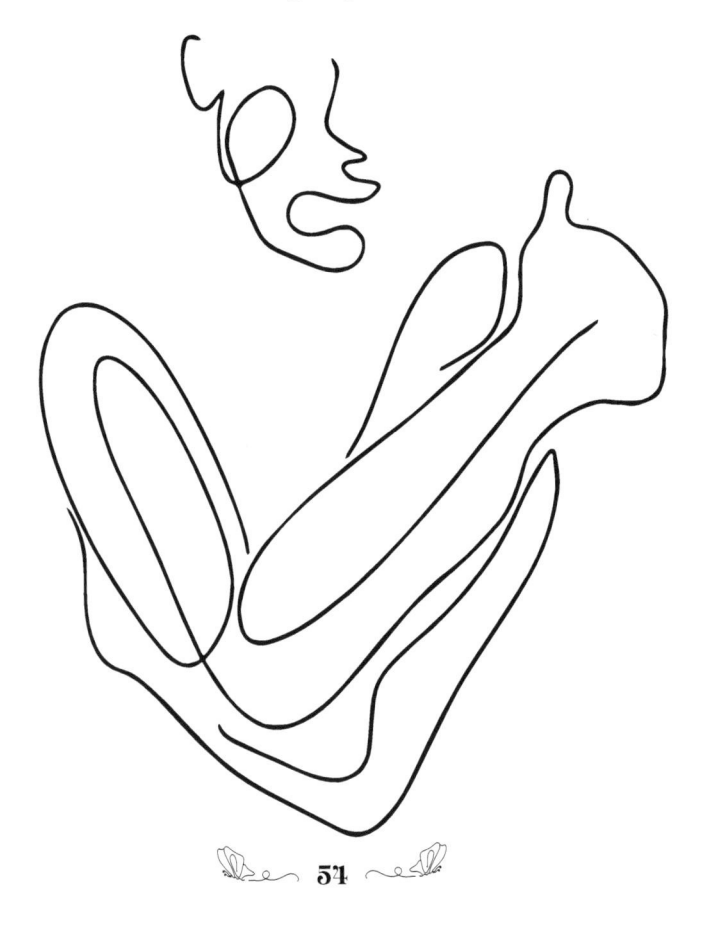

In My Cocoon

**No Power Struggles**

life will separate us
when it's time
we don't have to help her
enjoy me
be present with me

i have no interest in a power struggle
i want to let my guard down with you

Reyna Noriega

## Courage

loving takes courage
not luck
not instinct
you're not born less lovable
or less capable

but it takes courage
trust yourself
project your voice

In My Cocoon

## We Did It

when we were done
i felt full

you took no parts of me
i couldn't do without
i am still whole
i am still worth my weight
in diamonds

Reyna Noriega

## Doing Your Best

you haven't given yourself enough credit
yes you've been hurt
and disappointed
but you've grown so much
and you've been smart all along

people surprised you and disappointed you as
people tend to
but along the way
you made better choices
you listened
you watched patterns
compared words to actions

the last time you took a lover
you laughed
you felt free
you enjoyed yourself
you had no misconceptions about forever.
that was a shift, that was growth

before that, remember the time you spoke up?
you told him not to touch you
until he was ready

## In My Cocoon

to pour back into you
what you could feel him pulling from you

you said that, right in the middle of it

yes you imagined happy endings
yes you wanted more
but you were honest with yourself
and with him

the time you thought you gave too much
you didn't
you gave just enough.

you believed in him
but when he started to feed you excuses
you stood up and you asked,
at which point did he intend to act?
at which point did he plan to take responsibility?
and in forcing that honesty
everything unraveled,
just as it was meant to

you've been doing it from the start —
your best.

## Growth

*do you have the desire and capacity to love?*
-a question i would tell my younger self to ask

the epiphany comes as i give
my younger sister advice
for the first time in years
i reflect on all i've learned about men
and about love

i tell her
be assertive
be unapologetic about your needs
ask the questions you are afraid to ask

i tell her to live without expectation
don't try to hold water

flow

learn your boundaries
maintain them
respect them

In My Cocoon

## A Crossroads

you thought it would be that easy ?
*no*
here we go again
naturally you believe in magic
in fairytales
so you saw the potential
but you didn't get lost in it
maybe you should have waited
maybe you should've spoken up sooner
but this was inevitable

maybe you're making this harder
*no*
don't second guess yourself
you know how it feels to be held
to be safe
this one doesn't have the capacity for that
right now
maybe ever
let it go
let it flow

Reyna Noriega

## **Postponed**

like my move,
love is postponed
a welcomed distraction
but a distraction
is all it was

## In My Cocoon

This one was different. Special even. There were picnics, poems, and Polaroids. It was fun, it was respectful. It was liberating. But the shift came, subtly of course, but intuitively I knew it was a sign to behold. It was all in the non-verbals. So I asked, what were his intentions?

I heard something about fun, and a grey area, and him and his mental health being the priority right now.

And I respect it, the honesty. So I gifted myself some honesty as well. The old Reyna would've heard only parts of that speech. All the parts that were compliments to me, none of the parts that answered my question. The old Reyna would've convinced herself that it could be enough, for now at least, and that her patience would win his love.

The bottom line was, he didn't plan to be intentional right now and I couldn't blame him for it. No matter how fun, how romantic, it was only ever a quarantine fling. I could take it or leave it.

So I left it.

Reyna Noriega

## Save Your Words

save them for someone who cares…
save your poetry for the open hearts.

i take that back
speak your truth
who cares who listens
as long as you fly free

In My Cocoon

### Crush The Ego

humble him

it is not for malicious intent
humble him

stay in your power
stand your ground

crush the ego

you've spent your whole life
protecting everyone
but yourself

Reyna Noriega

## Thank You

i needed that
you were the last straw
the last bit of optimism
that things could just fall into place

that i could be oblivious
trust a stranger to lead

you are the last time
i can ever lie to myself,
betray myself

i don't want less than i deserve
not for now
not ever

## In My Cocoon

**The letter I won't send you:**

*I sensed the ego. The god complex. The narcissism. Even mentioned it in passing from time to time. But a little bit of that is healthy, no?*

*The truth is, you were a welcomed distraction. The universe and I both knew I was not ready. I was trying to put a band-aid on the gaping hole that pausing my dreams left.*

Reyna Noriega

### State Of Mind
Loving comes easy now,
writing comes easy
but the art,
does not
there is a block
caused by my anxious thoughts

In My Cocoon

## I Worry

when they go too soon
they haven't experienced the full range of me
my power
my heart
my strengths
it won't hurt them enough
to see me go

it used to tempt me to stay longer
to forgive betrayal
so they'd have a little more time
to get  to know me

but then i realized my energy speaks for me
my heart introduces me

i've been looking for an energy to match my own
my whole life
so i know
that once i'm gone
no matter how few and simple the moments

i will have left my mark

Reyna Noriega

## I Want To Be Un-perfect

i want to rewind the hands of time
and go back to the moment i learned
that perfection would win me love

so much performing
my back hurts
my heart feels shallow

i'm not perfect
i've repeated over and over
all my life
and yet still perform perfection
every day

this skin
it burns i want to rip it off
i want to feel naked
ignorant
free

i want to go back
to the moment i learned
perfection would win me love
and every moment thereafter
it's been reinforced

In My Cocoon

## Today Calls For Salsa

i want to hear colors
feel rhythms
smell life

it smells like freedom
it smells like euphoria
it smells like joy
it smells like love

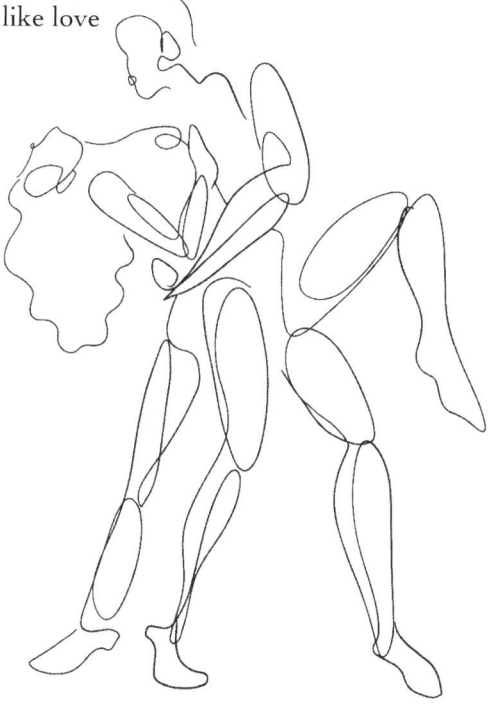

Reyna Noriega

## What Matters In A Home

light
lots of it
pouring in through the windows
and into our hearts

space.
doesn't matter how much space
it just matters that we can breath
and stretch
and expand

we...
who is this we i speak of

i guess it would be nice
to share responsibility with someone
to indulge in partnership
to never need to sleep alone

## In My Cocoon

*healing them is not your responsibility
and sometimes it's that simple.*

Reyna Noriega

do you just want it
or are you actually ready for it?
it requires a process
it requires preparation
it will take time
so you'll need a whole lot of patience

## In My Cocoon

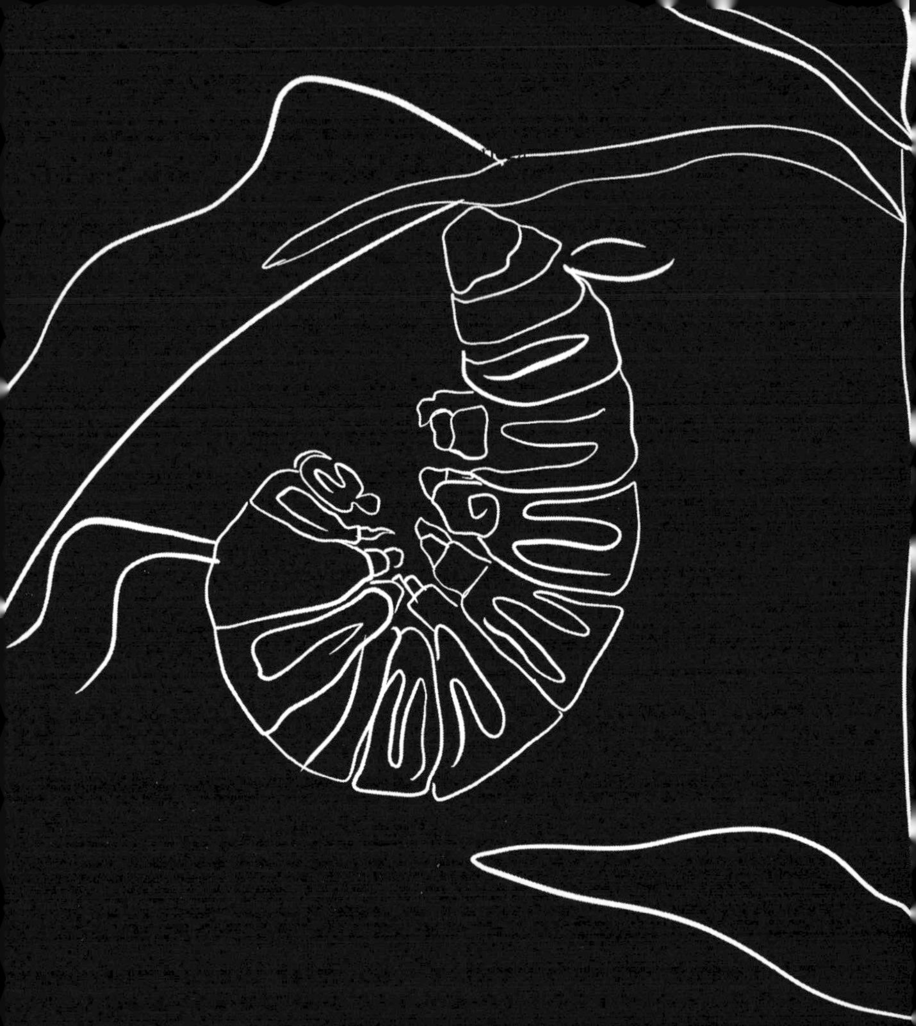

STAGE II:
It happens again.

One day, you realize the progress you have made was just that — Progress, not arrival.

There will come a time where you feel that familiar discomfort, as if you are shedding skin, outgrowing your body and your surroundings.

You will be forced inward, might as well get comfortable, strap yourself in.

Start forming your cocoon.

Reyna Noriega

In My Cocoon

## Is This It

too many times
i've asked myself
is this it?
the grand finale
the destiny

too many times
the universe has reminded me
it is just a lesson
or a blip in
the bigger picture

when will i learn
to just experience
and not get my hopes up

## Full Moon Release

thank you
for proving me wrong
for proving me right
for the space you occupied with me
just being
present
in the future when they tell me
there's no one
there's no one doing the work
i'll tell them they're wrong
or maybe i won't
the cynics wouldn't believe me
because i met the unicorn
i bathed in his light
and he was beautiful
so badly i wanted to cave
*this is fine, this can be enough*
i almost heard her scream it
and betray me
but we broke a curse tonight
under a full moon
and now there aren't many words
not even a song
that can fully capture what i feel

## In My Cocoon

because not many have made it this far
they've succumbed to the pessimism
imprisoned by their own expectations
but instead we fortified each other's wings
a true testimony to loving without possession
and i hope you soar
i let you go
when i realized you couldn't hold me
and now i am stronger for it

Reyna Noriega

## The Morning After

leaving you
my best chance
at a distraction
it hurts like hell
i feel your absence
in the pit of my gut
making the decision
i felt powerful
sitting in silence i feel—
not so sure

In My Cocoon

## The Purge

i want to stop the tears short
but this is a purge
you're potent
i need to get you out of my system
i am going to cry until i can't anymore
i am going to honor my feelings
i didn't expect this
what a beautiful surprise
gone after i'd only had a taste
a sample
it's not enough
but i have to tell myself that it is
if i don't stop
all these poems will be about you
but for now
i'm not done crying yet

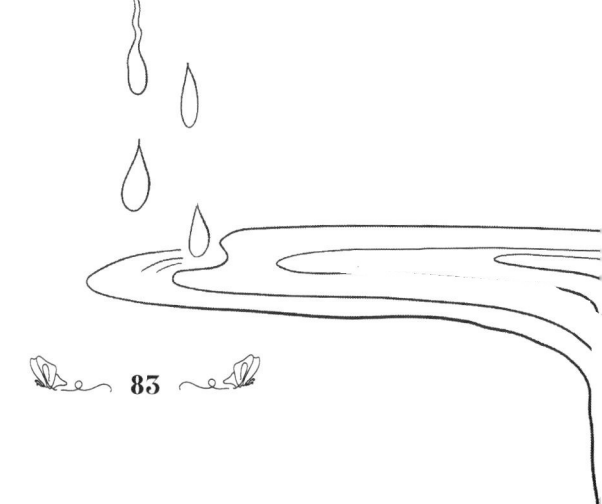

## Open Wound

is it easier for you
then it is for me in this moment?
i know i made this choice
and i'm proud of it
but the thought of not
just not
so much not
it aches
the peace i felt last night
was replaced with an ache this morning
i wished i was still waking up to possibility
this is not my higher self thinking
she knows there will be so much love
so so much
it will be strong
secure
never ending
but i am processing…
i'll get there
i know
but we left too soon
so it hurts today
and i hope it will be better tomorrow

In My Cocoon

## Morning Mourning

i acknowledge i am in mourning
grieving
and with it comes its obsessive ticks
i've muted you
to trick my brain into thinking
you've called
you've reached out
i just haven't been notified.
and break my own heart when i check
are you watching my social media?
*yes*.
what does it mean?
*nothing*.
it'll pass.
i forget to run the instant replay for 5 minutes,
then 10
get lost in a task for an hour
soon it'll be days
how is it for you i wonder?
i'll likely never know

Reyna Noriega

## I'm Growing

i want to keep growing
i will forever be blooming
i want someone to bloom with
someone that can hold me
through the transitions
catch parts i may have missed
lovingly help me
correct course

In My Cocoon

## Day 3

i feel reality starting to creep in
and prevail over my romanticism
i no longer have any desire
to fill in the blanks of your speech
with assumptions that you
wanted me so badly
you feared so deeply
you put up a wall
because the fact remains
it wasn't deep enough
it wasn't strong enough
or you would be here

Reyna Noriega

## Day 4

i barely remember your smile
or smell
but i still feel your eyes on me

the burn stings less today

In My Cocoon

## Who Are We

who are we
to argue with the universe
if she says we are ready?
suit up
lace your boots
get ready
sometimes the choice
is above us

Reyna Noriega

## Enough About You

what about me?
i've released so much
i feel so much lighter
so much surer of the space i occupy
so much surer of the body
i am expanding into
its been a few days but already,
you wouldn't recognize me

In My Cocoon

*i can't wait until i forget you*

Reyna Noriega

## **No Time**

a few weeks
and we amassed so many memories
i'm often surprised when a new one
pops up
i decide i want my whole life to feel like this
all my future loves to feel like this
like time is running out
like the world is on fire
and all we have left to do
is love

In My Cocoon

## So Much

so much i would normally do
to keep my mind moving forward
but the whole world
has been placed on pause
i guess it is time
to wrap myself
in my cocoon
be still with myself

## The Catalyst

i'm on the verge of a new awakening
perhaps i needed this
before leaving the comfort of my home country
i needed this
before truly sharing myself with someone
in isolation i met my first bloom
this time i am blossoming again
without a place to hide
my tears,
my mistakes,
my discomfort all on display
i'm learning so much
it's hurting so much
but i must carry on

In My Cocoon

## Love

love will always be central
i can accept that
all the lesson i thought
i learned before
they seem silly now
they weren't the lesson
the one that would
finally make me look within
the one that would
finally drive home the fact that
there was no magic coming
there is just the magic inside
that illuminates
and it is up to me to choose
someone who will protect that light
shine with me
light the whole world up

Reyna Noriega

## Share

just share
with mistakes
unfinished
un-perfect
just share!
you'll get better
you'll get more honest
give yourself a starting point
just share

In My Cocoon

## Day 4.5

i don't care.
i am looking in the mirror
i'm incredible
i am remembering my power and light
good riddance

## How to get over a heartbreak in 4 days

Ultimately, you are on a path to realize you are not actually heartbroken. Your expectations have been shattered, your ego a little bruised, but your heart is beating. You will be fine

Day 1: Give yourself 24 hours to grieve. This is not the time to distract yourself. Cry. Let it out. Watch the movies, read the poems. Write the text (but don't send). Sleeping will be hard, eating will feel pointless and unsatisfying. Stay hydrated and brace yourself.

Day 2: Grief will spill over and brown into anger. This is where you may experience and work through feelings of entitlement. You ask questions like, how could this happen to ME? Be sure to counteract these questions and feelings with the reminder this is happening FOR you. No one is yours, but the lessons are and they lead to your betterment.

Day 3: Honor yourself, your journey and the experience. Find gratitude in all the experience has given you. It is yours to keep. Through gratitude, you may come to realize that what the situation offered you was only a temporary filler for your ultimate wish.

Day 4: It may still start out a little rocky but remember who you are.
Everything you likely miss about this person is in your head, but everything you know and love about yourself is real and waiting to be acknowledged by you.

You will be delicate, be weary of the content you consume. Social media may not be the best place. Sad songs, not too helpful. Try to replenish you heart, mind, and spirit with all it needs to get back to working for you.

If it still hurts, repeat step one to four until healed.

Reyna Noriega

*A proverb:*

don't spend your life waiting for people to
regret how they treated you

maybe they didn't treat you that badly
maybe they were only meant to reveal
your codependency
or inflated expectations

i don't mean to blame,
perhaps i'm liberated
releasing you from a mental prison

In My Cocoon

## Unless

i'm doing the work
so that we can eventually unite
you better be doing the same.

logic
logic has no place in love
unless-
you don't love me
you don't want to see me rise
you don't want to light a fire within me
you can't be your best with me
you can't change the world with me
we can't grow together
we can't create together

if that is the case,
by all means be logical
otherwise-
spare me your excuses
and love me

Reyna Noriega

## Keep Shedding

oh hey you
nice to meet you
again
you're different than i remember
softer, but stronger some how
i see that you've shed some dead weight
broken through some chains
you stand a bit straighter too
what's your secret?
confronting the ghosts?
i bet it was painful
but you did it
i'm proud of you
keep shedding
keep cocooning
until you are the butterfly

you're almost there

In My Cocoon

## Wandering

my mind wanders
i think back,
ticket booked
plans made
i was ready to go
but the universe had other plans
i am disappointed
i am anxious
but i will see
what this space in time brings
what clarity it offers

Reyna Noriega

## Internal Embrace

pouring so much into myself
i feel like i might pop
boiling over with love and goodness
magic shooting from my fingertips
"i love you"
i tell her several times a day
and i feel the internal
*-the eternal*
embrace

In My Cocoon

## Day 5

you texted
an olive branch maybe?
do i respond?
or let you sweat?
revenge for what i've been through these last 5 days
no no no
i don't do that any more
i've released you
i don't want to instigate your anxiety
to sooth my ego
my kindness is free
i have enough to share with you
with brevity
because i need more time
with me

## My All

shall i write the book today ?
paint the picture?
what will i create
or read
or dream
back to giving me
all of me
and the options are endless

In My Cocoon

## Focus

i need focus
i mean i'm pretty good at focusing
until a notification...
...as i was saying
i get a lot done daily
i draw a lot
um...
i'd like to read more
finish my novel

i think i could do that
if i focused more
on one thing
longer
but my attention span
it gets shared with so much
i can change that i think

hold that thought
i know i must be
forgetting something
on my to do list

## This Is A Love Story

whether or not there is a lover involved
the loving is eternal
and most of it
circulated within me

In My Cocoon

## Daydreaming

i see myself sitting
by a wide wide window
light is pouring in
floor to ceiling
it is not so bright today
it's been raining
there is a mood in the air
it is thick
it is carrying the scent
of new dreams imagined

i needed this moment to myself
the book is taking me away
to another place
another time
it is almost lustful
and i smile

i realize
that is what i want
more than anything—
peace

Reyna Noriega

## Heal to Reveal

you keep asking "how will i know"
heal.
heal!
heal and you will know

you are divinely protected and guided
every experience
has been preparing you
to focus inward
strengthen your bond with self
so that self can speak
so that self can guide

In My Cocoon

## It Works Out

stop stressing the outcome
leave room to be surprised
it has always worked out
it will always work out
better than
you could've constructed
if you were in control

## Magic

i take back what i said before
i do want the fairytale
my life is a damn fairytale
if you don't want to contribute to the magic
you're not welcome here

it leaves an air of uncertainty
when you come without magic
when you pretend not to see my own

In My Cocoon

## Indecisive

i know what i want
it is sad
i must act like i don't
because you're unsure
i won't do it
i'll remove myself instead

Reyna Noriega

## The Prophecy

a Prophet
am i?
as a child i can remember
thinking
dreaming
imagining
the life i now live

thanks for the courage to follow the whispers
the skills to see it through
i am almost there

In My Cocoon

*shhh...*

don't distract me
i'm relearning lessons
i thought i already mastered
i need to get them right this time

Reyna Noriega

## Self Healing

perhaps the hardest job
you will ever have
will be healing yourself
nursing the wounds living has caused
the third degree burns of failure
stitching the heart back together
but when you can see them
all as lessons
strengths
you will rise again

In My Cocoon

## Dreaming

and in that dream
few things are certain
i will be happy
i will feel safe
i will laugh
i will dance

other things are uncertain
but a part of the magic
a part of the allure
to keep dreaming

Reyna Noriega

## Choose Wings

vulnerability is cool
self reflection is better
revealing your wounds to the world
can also be a crutch
an escape
all "look what's happened to me"
and not enough
"lets do the work to get beyond this"
i thought i was special
for tapping into that vulnerability
until i learned accountability
until i learned to do the work
you know what i consider "cool" now?

you will never know more about me
than i know of me
you will never be able to tell me
who i am
my self awareness has liberated me
it has given me new wings
where there were once anchors

In My Cocoon

it is so beautiful
yet so painful
to still love and respect
the ones you've left

— i'm proud of you

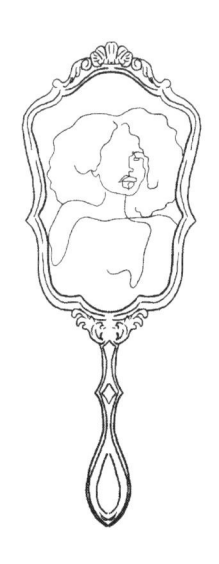

Reyna Noriega

it's not so mysterious
it's not so elusive
it just is

*—love just is*

In My Cocoon

## A New Normal

there will be no returning
a true test to my resilience
my dreams will have to adapt
my living
all of it

we are being stripped
of everything we thought mattered
and all that will be left
all that will remain
is the one thing
we cannot lose
*love*

Reyna Noriega

## A Year From Now

i will look back
and again see growth
i could not have imagined
i did pulled the weeds
but missed a bunch
it wasn't lazy
just not thorough enough
and now
as i get on my knees again
i dig and pull until my nails bleed
i clean and restore
until it is safe
to eat from this ground

In My Cocoon

## Subtle Changes

my hips move more
my belly fills with laughter
i stand a bit straighter
all these subtle changes
i only notice when looking in retrospect
it was worth it
the pain
the tears
the leaving
the stretching
it was worth it
i love this person that stares at me
i know her so intimately

Reyna Noriega

## Excited

to keep loving
to keep learning
to keep evolving
i can approach the uncertainty
of the future
with anxiety
or i can continue to adapt
and forge my own narrative
the uncertainty
the unknown,
it leaves room
for the universe
to surprise me
it has always sent me
better
than my human brain can conceive
better
than i thought i deserved

*In My Cocoon*

## Do Away With Labels

we don't use words like bad or evil
we call it healing
learning
give them space to evolve in your mind
free them
free yourself

do away with the labels
it does them no good
it freezes time
it blocks grace

you aren't required to stick around
for the process
you aren't expected
to do the work for them
but--

free them
and you too
will be free

Reyna Noriega

## Anticipation

i'm just so overjoyed for new
i deserve so much
i will receive so much
i've claimed it
and now i wait—
not anxiously
not checking the clock
not comparing my harvest
i work and wait
and prepare myself

In My Cocoon

## New

i like this new version
honoring my sensitive side
mourning the death of my expectations
but i've matured enough to not allow myself
to dwell in that space
i stay present
what is
is all there is
what could be
is a myth
and none of it is a reflection of my worth
only i decide that

Reyna Noriega

## About *Him*

i guess i haven't mentioned him
but now that my feelings are out and honest
they don't seem so big and scary
i loved him
that is a fact
i admire him
that is still a fact
i would've loved
to meet him again
these are all facts
but my heart is open
open to new
open to bigger
open to the present
i can now fully love another
without it feeling like there is a secret
between us
as deep as the atlantic
that separates us
my past is past
my present is a temporary gift
i won't miss it
like all the days i spent
 missing him

## In My Cocoon

i'm more aligned with myself
i no longer want to run to him
i no longer need him to save me

Reyna Noriega

## People

people matter
and you better
start showing up for them
if you want someone to show up for you

give what you hope to receive
put more loving energy into this world
everyone won't understand
they may not have the capacity
to return the favor
but that isn't the point

In My Cocoon

## Choose More

don't let scarcity mindset
have you disrespecting your boundaries
tolerating disrespect from people
staying in positions that make your gut turn
because you think that if you walk away,
the world will crumble
the opportunities will cease
you will look back
at all you've entertained
for far too long
and wonder why

Reyna Noriega

## Home Is

home is transient
because it travels with you
geography means nothing
cultivate your inner home
and it will follow you wherever you go

# In My Cocoon

*"i'm like shedding right now
it's really nasty and not cute
but so necessary"*

*— Karla*

## Why

and sometimes i just have to ask
why
why would you want to be loved all fumbly
by someone who doesn't understand
the magic they have
the opportunity they hold
all the prayers you are answering
just by being in their presence

## Don't Settle

it is a no
unless it resembles my dreams
or better
in love
in work
in life
in home

Reyna Noriega

## I Am The One

i shudder
thinking back to the times
i prayed someone would see the magic in me
i'm glad i never begged
but even when i would retreat
pride still in tact
in the quiet moments
i would hope and pray and plead
that they'd realize
i was the one
for the job
for the place
for their love

i am the one
one of one
and for that reason
i pray and beg for nothing
but for more opportunities
meant especially for me

## Contentment

i am happy
therefore i am not looking for anything
i am not longing for anything
but i welcome more joy
more abundance
more love
more showing up fully present
fully enamored
with life

Reyna Noriega

## Come Live Here

i welcome
*love*
that wants to grow
i welcome
*intimacy*
that wants to stay
i welcome
*care*
that is genuine and pure
i welcome
*passion*
that fills my whole body with heat
i welcome
*communication*
that combats my anxiety
come live here

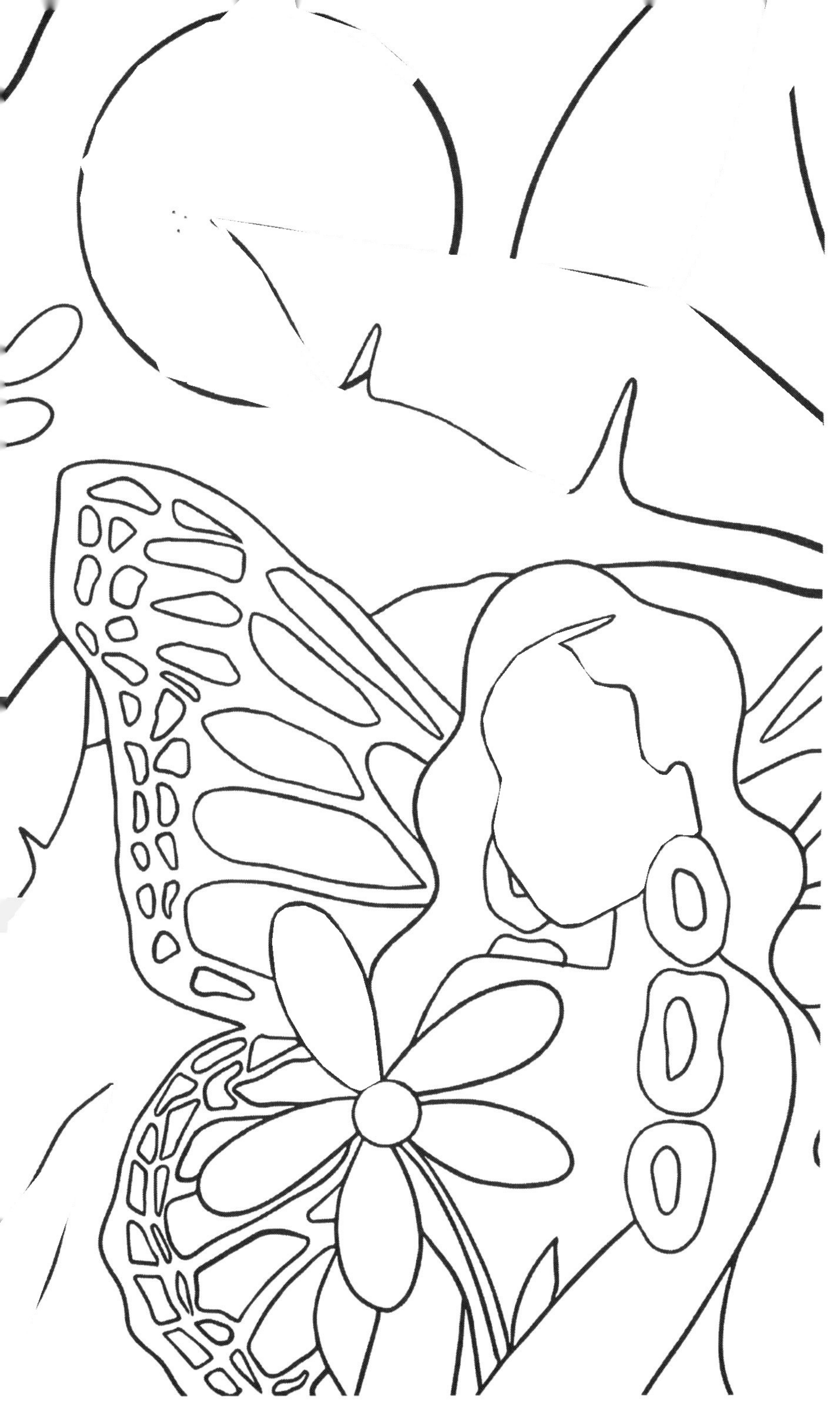

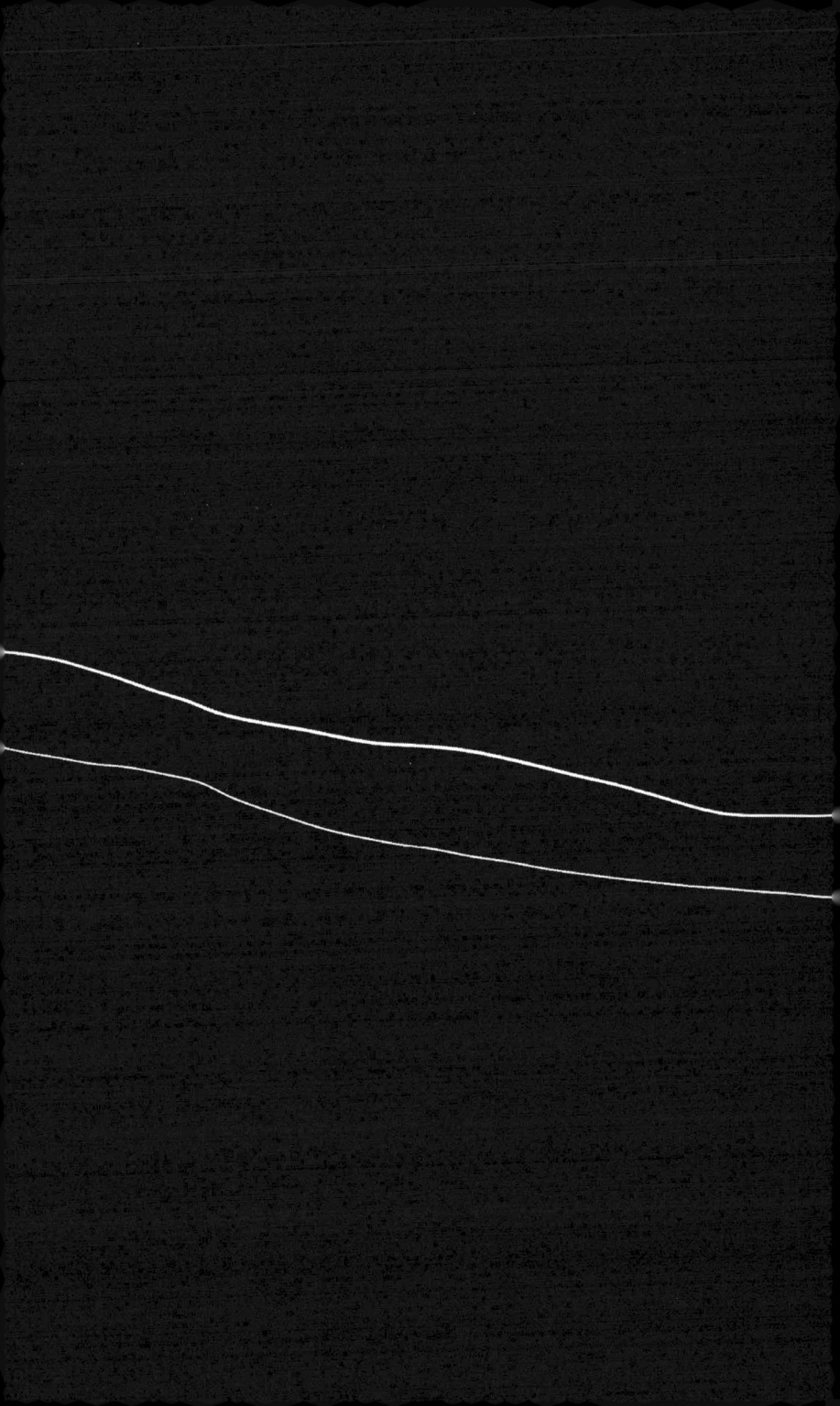

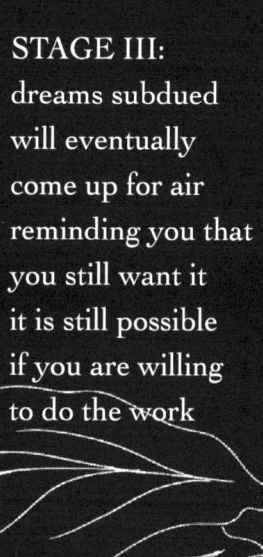

STAGE III:
dreams subdued
will eventually
come up for air
reminding you that
you still want it
it is still possible
if you are willing
to do the work

Reyna Noriega

In My Cocoon

## We Got Us

i'm anxious today
i'm taking steps backward
worrying
considering my options
be still
i've got you
i'm here
i won't leave
i've got you
look in the mirror
we've got us
when nothing else is guaranteed,
know that
we. got. us

Reyna Noriega

## Self-Healing

i can break my own cycles
i don't need anyone to come in
so that i can rewrite my past
undo my wrongs
and mistakes
feel the satisfaction
of receiving a new ending
i can break my own cycles
something big is coming
something new and sweet
and it won't heal the wounds
that were there before
i will do that
for myself

In My Cocoon

## Conflict

I have to sit in it
Face it with you
Why is this even harder than sharing my body with you?
But I'm sitting here
On the brink of tears because I'm not sure how to separate my reality from my expectations, not sure how to start the conversation that will lead to a resolution
One where we are stronger
more capable of communicating our needs
Meeting in the middle

I start
Trying my best to sound confident.
I've never had to do this. Never gotten to this point.
It was always perfect, and then over. And I am grateful I have stopped trying to escape into fairytales.
While I was manifesting the perfect partner I realized that I needed to wish the same of myself. My ability to communicate.

I inhale knowing that I am divinely guided and my intentions are pure, and although I haven't had the opportunity to practice with a partner, I am ready to start now.

"It hurts me when you don't show up for me the way I expect you to, but I realize I may not have articulated what those expectations are."
I look at you expecting to see the wall, the annoyance, the distance, the shielding, defensiveness, anything that will make me swallow my words and storm off
"Forget it" I'd say, "you don't care."

But instead, there's slight traces of a smile.
As if you've been waiting for me to say these things for a long time.
You encourage me to keep going
You let me talk until it's all out
You hold my hand to let me know you're with me, not going anywhere.

"I had no idea my actions affected you that way, Now that I know, I'll do all that I can

## In My Cocoon

to make sure you never feel like that again"
Not wanting things to feel one sided I say
"How can I better show up for you"
"This, keep letting me know how you feel. Don't ever fear my reaction. Your truth matters to me"
And I melt against you, shaken to my core.

A vision so vivid,
I know what I must work on next.

*Embrace the Conflict, understanding is born there.*

Reyna Noriega

## **Values**

the new wealth
is strength
stability
longevity
safety

the new luxury
is peace

In My Cocoon

## What Matters Most

here's the new plan,
forget making a list of qualities
find someone you can talk to
lets start there

## Too Busy

i want to be too busy communicating and
figuring things out with my partner to need
to consult with anyone else
i need to be so intuned with my soul
i don't need to compare notes
cross references
i just need to listen

In My Cocoon

*i'm not in a rush to find another,
i want to find me.*

## Reflections

I realize now that my dreams were once filled with too much of that wanty, needy, dreamy stuff. To some extent I wanted to be saved. Saved from the responsibility of discernment, and of making mistakes. I don't blame myself, this life is not easy. Why should I want to work for love? Why should I want to dissect my own trauma to better understand my loving style. But I look back and realize I am in my mid 20's and I have never argued with anyone. I have loved, I have enjoyed, and at the first sight of conflict, I have left. I took difficulty as a sign we weren't meant to be. And maybe

## In My Cocoon

we were not, but that isn't to be decided by conflict.

I had no boundaries, no voice to express my expectations. I was just enamored with romance, and gone once the fog cleared and disillusionment came.

Don't be like me.
The most painful realization came from saying to myself, "maybe it's me". Maybe love hasn't come because I am no where near ready to nurture it. Real love.

And I want that, don't I? So I must be willing to face my demons.

Reyna Noriega

## Letting Go To Receive

relinquishing control
letting everything come to me with ease
letting my guides do the work for me
while i focus inward
so that i can continue to build myself up
and meet my blessings as i'm ready for them.

In My Cocoon

## **Oversaturated**

overstimulated
i've read too much
thought too much
worried too much

stillness
is much needed
along with recalibration
quiet

## Standards

why do we want the attention
the admiration
of people who don't even like themselves?
it is a losing battle
and not your purpose
teach them how to love themselves
by honoring yourself
and walking away when they would love nothing more
than to see you beg for their attention
and beg for their approval

In My Cocoon

## Seeking Calm

i wish i knew
how to flip the switch
to my relaxed state
i've seen my dreams unfold
but when i'm tense
and anxious
and trying to foretell outcomes
it can be so hard to get there
i would love nothing more
than to just sit back,
relax
enjoy this show

Reyna Noriega

i've been preparing my whole life for this
this is everything i've ever wanted and more

i feel it before it comes
so i know it is on the way

*—gratitude*

In My Cocoon

## Logging Off...

the ignorance
it triggers you
why do you continue to read?
you know their minds won't change
or their biases
their privilege comes with rose tinted glasses
they won't come off voluntarily
don't digest too much of it

Reyna Noriega

## Where Is The Leak

how do i stop
the good feelings
from fading away?
it feels like
all it takes
is a few days
and i'm back
in the mirror
chanting

*i am enough*
*here is enough*

where is the leak?
where am i allowing
energy in
that doesn't belong?

In My Cocoon

## Stay Present

daydreaming sometimes morphs
into overthinking
one second you're thinking of all you want
and would love to have
next you're being tricked into thinking what
you have now is not enough
this is why i must stay present

Reyna Noriega

## **Endurance**

there are no cheat codes
so we're better off
building our endurance
for the long haul

In My Cocoon

### Art ~ Pain

there's almost no pain left
no longing
i can feel it evaporating
i've made so much peace
healed so many wounds
i hope there is more to write about
and if there isn't,
it's ok
i will have made my contribution
i will have made room for new writers
i won't sit in trauma
for the sake of making art

Reyna Noriega

## A Language

making art
can't be about making a lot of stuff
it's about feeling a lot of things
and needing a language
to communicate in

In My Cocoon

## Go Deeper

this pain is surface level
go deeper
there's more than you have dared touch

Reyna Noriega

## Let's Deep Dive

let's take the plunge
into the deep dark corners of our minds
where pain has become welts
that still hurt to the touch
filled with all the bad things
that have happened
and will happen
and might happen again
where the lost wishes deteriorate
where it reeks of disappointment
heartbreak
the first betrayal of our mothers,
or fathers
someone or something
we thought could do no wrong
let's walk through this
grab my hand,
i know the memories this will unearth
will be painful

## In My Cocoon

but please don't shield your eyes
it is time to see
this will help us answer the hard questions
why do we want this so bad?
what do we run away from?
how can we be still with ourselves?

*we can do this.*

Reyna Noriega

## Letter to my inner child

Please tell me why you're sad. Please tell me what hurts you. The star child, the optimist, which experiences tainted you? Please tell me so I can let you know we are okay now. I have taken care of us as best as I can and right now I'm trying to do better. Because we deserve peace.

I know you thought everything would be as beautiful as your parents love, as beautiful as a ballet. I know the betrayal cut you raw and when you realized the world wouldn't

In My Cocoon

be that kind, the feeling was overwhelming. We watched so many romances, fell in love to so many love songs and mistakenly believed life would also be that kind. And it wasn't.

We expected others to care for us, put our needs first, and that wasn't always the case.

So many books we got lost in. Traveling to mythical places, we saw magic everywhere. We decided in those pages, we wanted to make magic too. I want you to know the magic was always within. It was there when you were singled out, when your eyebrows were too thin, when you couldn't understand why your thighs were so much bigger than theirs or why you couldn't run as fast.

You were so special, we are so special. Your existence blesses so many people. You gave your Abuela the will to live, for you. You were that special before you even took your first breath.

I see you. Pigtails, and hair bubbles. In your favorite overalls. I see us at the park with the orange tubes. Innocence still in tact. I give you permission. To release yourself of blame for what happened when you were too young to understand. You don't have to overcompensate with perfection anymore. Flaws and all, you are perfect. You can reclaim whatever innocence was lost.

Look at us, even now, putting all the pieces together again by ourselves. And perhaps that is why we so desperately anticipated a love that could seemingly reset all the shame, guilt, and disappointment. I want us to be free of that so that we can enjoy a love that is pure and mutual, and free. We won't crumble if we let someone love us. We won't break if they lie and leave.

You are impeccable. Your smile, your charisma, your aura. You have been brightening up rooms for almost 3 decades. A diamond. I'm sorry for not telling you sooner. We wanted to fit in even though the squeezing hurt. Now I give you permission to stand out, or help me and walk with me. I want to thank you for carrying me here. You don't have to prove yourself. I'm looking at you and you are so special. All slanted eyes and wide grins, round face and puffy cheeks. You can now demand the respect you deserve.

You were never "too" anything, besides maybe too good for this world.

We walk together now. I've got you. To me, you are everything. You have wings like a beautiful dove. Use them when you need them. We can escape this world whenever.

I need to ask a favor of you. I promise to support you through this part because it can get scary. I need you to let go, let loose, fall in love. Allow us to enjoy love, and both emotional and physical intimacy. I've got you and we will not break just because we let someone in to our castle. Together we will welcome only worthy visitors who wish to bring beauty to our kingdom. I need you to let them know you. I will make sure they love, honor, and respect you. Your instincts are strong and correct. They have been all of your life. Our guard must come down, as I do my part to learn our boundaries.

I'm going to take care of you and stay with you, but I want us to be able to share our magic with someone else. I need you to trust yourself so we can approach new love with strength, confidence, and a strong sense of what we want. I won't rush you. I'm here for you. I will work through this with you until we get it right. The fairytales we've watched and read, we deserve that and we are ready for that. Because regardless of the outcome, we have each other.

I love you so much. I'll never judge or abandon you.

— *Love, Reyna*

## In My Cocoon

*There's always space for more love.*

Reyna Noriega

## The Pause

the whole world pauses
as my mind charges on full speed
it makes me a bit dizzy
i need to catch my footing

but i charge on
it is again
time to heal

In My Cocoon

## Please Heal

my evolving self is sad for you
sad that you are in the same place
i left you 2 books ago
still lying
still manipulating
still clinging to a god awful God complex
that will prevent you from reaching any divinity
you can't hear me anymore
i can't speak to you directly anymore
but i'm sending love

Reyna Noriega

i don't have to
think the worst of you.
i can just
not
think of you.

In My Cocoon

## The Conflict Is Internal

they cannot steal what is rightfully yours
if it feels like happiness, success, or love
is fleeting
consider perhaps,
it is not being taken from you
maybe there is work you can still do
to understand how to make it last
the universe doesn't want us to suffer
we prolong our suffering with defiance,
refusing to surrender
failing to take the lesson as a gift
there are secrets in all of our struggles
in grief
in heartache
and the test is,
will you go inward?
examine your triggers
take the opportunity to find even a droplet
of gratitude
or will you curse at the sky
compare your struggle
resort to anger
lethargy

Reyna Noriega

*choose to rise like the phoenix you were meant to be every time*
                              *-rise*

In My Cocoon

*life is exhausting
and i think i'd sleep better
in your arms.*

Reyna Noriega

## I'll Find Another

and i'll find better

apartment rejections remind me
patience
surrender
it all works out in due time

In My Cocoon

## Keep Planting Seeds

you may be in a waiting period
something that feels like limbo
it may feel as though all your efforts
have been futile
keep planting seeds
keep getting to know yourself
grow
challenge yourself
all of your blessings
are on their way to you
be ready
in an instant all those seeds
may sprout
and when the world finally opens their eyes
they will see that you have cultivated
the most beautiful garden
keep planting seeds
don't wait to be noticed

Reyna Noriega

## Growing Pains

there were fun parts
of growing and finding myself
mood boards for my higher self
her room and space
her style
it was fun creating unapologetically
feeling free
creating self care routines
more music
more rest
more boundaries
it was not fun
getting there
looking in the mirror
*crying*
forgiving myself
for all the times i believed i wasn't enough
for all the wrongs i committed
not acting out of love
losing people
*ouch*
walking away from things
*ouch*

## In My Cocoon

saying no
*ouch*
showing up
when i wanted nothing more
than to run to my bed
under the covers
and hide
but instead having to stand naked
so exposed to the world
in this new skin
scary as hell
but it was worth it

Reyna Noriega

### For Representation

i want my work
to always be accessible
to the women that look like me
the women that share my experiences
the women that need the reminder
they are full, whole, beautiful beings
i want my work to be accessible
to the little girls that will become
those women

as i grow,
this must remain.

In My Cocoon

## Commit to you

at some point
you have to stop
letting fear
get in the way
of what would
make you happy
if there is anyone
in this world
you should be able to trust
to make your
dreams come true,

it should be you

Reyna Noriega

why are you still obsessing over something you've released?

*stop*

stop romanticizing people that aren't good for you.

In My Cocoon

## Equilibrium Needed

a burst of clarity
ever notice how you romanticize everything?
once there's a spark
your mind weaves an intricate story
only you are privy to
this takes you high
so high
floating on imaginary ecstasy
and when it deviates
or there isn't anything new to keep fueling
this high
then comes the anxiety
the anxiety has you writing a horror story
maybe not that bad
but tragedy
it can go from
dream to nightmare
in a flash
find your equilibrium

Reyna Noriega

## Come and Go

hi stress
hi anxiety
overthinking, you're here too?
welcome
thanks for spending some time with me
nice of you to come
just know
you can't stay here
so pass through
tell me your secrets
and keep going
you can't live here anymore

In My Cocoon

## Do It

do it scared.
do it unqualified.
do it "not ready".
do it alone
do it with help
as long as you *do*

Reyna Noriega

## Soon

i look forward to not caring
i look forward to being fully healed
not even a scar as evidence

this part of the healing process
sucks.

its raw
i'm tender
i'm working through it

In My Cocoon

## Prepare

if not now, when?
when is the wrong question
if not now until then i am
in preparation
i am growing
i am healing
i am reflecting
so that when it comes
it will be a blessing
not another lesson

Reyna Noriega

## Be Yourself

i know it seems like
everyone but you
has the secret sauce
but all you're seeing
is that they've perfected theirs
and now it's time
to tend to yours

## New Moon

old thoughts
arise and demand
release
whatever was missed
whatever was ignored
will be dealt with
a new relationship
with self
will emerge
and space will be made for new
for better
for love

Reyna Noriega

## Get Through It

that thing you're going through
that feels like your downfall
that thing you're going through
that feels like the end
weather the storm
stay the course

it is priming you for your awakening
preparing you to shed skin
and to grow
do not be so afraid of the shedding
you stay small
you stay stuck

keep going

In My Cocoon

## A Dream

how nice would it be
to meet someone
and hear them say
"i have been doing so much
internal work
just to be sure i'd be ready
for someone like you,
so that i would know i deserve
someone like you,
and so that i could be sure
i were more than enough
for someone like you,"
to be someone's answered prayer—
for them to bring peace rather than ego
what a breath of fresh air

Reyna Noriega

## Bilingual

in the language of my father
so much pride
but also shame
that it's not enough
never will be
it makes me tongue tied
but if i never try
if i never make mistakes
let them correct me
the only time i'll ever speak
like this
the way i can in private
in the shower
like a telenovela star
will be when i've had too much sangria
i say i'm doing it for Barcelona
but really it's for me
my identity

In My Cocoon

## Sometimes

the things i'd like to say
feel repetitive
like maybe i'm not the only one that's saying
things
but their words don't carry my intentions
so i continue to create
i continue to paint
i continue to be
the embodiment of all i'd like to see

Reyna Noriega

what is my mask?
perfection perhaps

In My Cocoon

### ~~Love~~ Lust Is a Forest Fire

i don't want romance
too many times i've seen it sizzle
and burn
and then dissipate
fires are a marvel to the eye
but they carry no intentions
besides to devour
to consume
they don't care if you can breathe
they don't care if you survive their fury
they just burn

## Loud Thoughts

oh is it 5 o'clock?
perfect time for an existential crisis

will they stop caring?
will the art get boring?
will i run out of ideas?

In My Cocoon

## Quiet

just for tonight
i'm turning it off
the noise
the intentions
the inner work
the reflection
the thoughts of you
the never ending to do list

## Waiting

the person working on themselves
the person happy with themselves
the person making room for me
come soon please

In My Cocoon

## No Substitutes

if i still want what's not promised to me
what's not good for me
am i really ready?

## Protect Your Peace

don't welcome people into your space just because you are lonely
don't welcome nostalgia into your brain knowing it leads to overthinking
and all the thoughts that allow you to choose familiarity over your boundaries.

In My Cocoon

## Find Your Voice

in my writing
i speak to me
i've seen the danger
in thinking
you can speak for everyone
or that your message can be for everyone

although i believe
in the power and beauty
in everyones journey
all lessons won't be the same
it can never be one size fits all

stop buying their "coaching"
stop falling for their way
carve your own path
i hope to lead you to you
through me

## *Always*

i'll always come back to you
i say to myself
my inner child
my higher self
i'll always come back to you
back to alignment
no matter how far
the world might make me drift

In My Cocoon

the moons in cancer
the sky is grey
my mind is on you
- *drifting*

## Refill

you were honest with yourself
you set a boundary
it felt good.

why are you second guessing yourself?

*loneliness*

what are you not feeding yourself?

In My Cocoon

### Rise Together

i'm getting better with time
so when you decide to merge paths
you better be ready
trains moving fast
we are ascending
our wildest dreams are within reach
i won't stop until mine are actualized
i'll do the same for you

Reyna Noriega

## Imagine

all my fantasies include
loving someone
who loves himself
the way i love myself
the way i demand my growth
imagine the overflow of love
imagine the growth

In My Cocoon

## Can't Wait

can't wait to tell you
all the work i did to get ready for you
how i almost gave up
how i had to start over again and again
i can't wait to tell you it was so—
so worth it

Reyna Noriega

## Moving

packing again
refining my belongings
purging myself of clutter
what new beginnings await i wonder —
new plants for sure
new air
new views
new neighbors
what will they teach me

In My Cocoon

*Pain*-t

i do a good job of disguising my pain
sometimes it feels like running
*not my stuff*
the traumas that come from living
the pain that weighs on me
from the misjudgment
the maltreatment of my people
my people are Black
left bleeding out in streets like animals
rotting in prisons
slavery in disguise
my pain is for humans
told they are not worthy of a home
convinced they earned their struggle
while wealth is hoarded
by little balding white men
that is why i hide behind a paint brush
add as much color as i can
to distract from the black and blue bruising
of our hearts

Reyna Noriega

## Your Wildest Dreams

you can make your wildest dreams come true
i love the way my dreams seduce me
the way they whisper in my ear
brush against me
and challenge me
will you act on it?
will you fight for us?
they remind me i have the power
they also remind me it won't be easy

In My Cocoon

## Locked Doors

my home is sacred
more sacred than a temporary fix
for loneliness
it's human to feel lonely
it's human to want
but i know
you can only stay
if you'll add to the space
energetically
because if my home
ceases to feel like a safe space
if it becomes a prison
rather than the birthplace of my ideas
and i let you pollute my body
what do i have left
where do i turn

Reyna Noriega

## Something New

i'm excited
it's smaller
it's different
i'm nervous
but i see so much joy here
color
it will be different
i need different

In My Cocoon

## Thank You

to anyone
that has awoken
anything
within me
thank you
whether it was good or bad
it's beautiful
i feel beautiful
and one way or another
it's because of the mirror you held up to me

## Demands

if it's in writing
then it is a promise i must keep to myself
no more
no more of that weepy yearning stuff
it makes you grasp onto fairytales
forget yourself and your demands
you are so one of a kind
we can and we will gate-keep
who has access
i am not afraid to offend
to distance myself
if it means standing in my power
owning my rarity
claiming the space i want to take up
i won't whisper it quietly like a plea
not anymore
i'm not asking

In My Cocoon

## I Choose Me

i've tip-toed around people
that weren't afraid to lose me
for far too long
only here to absorb
and suck
whatever they can from me
so please understand
if i seem unafraid of choosing me over you
if that offends you
makes you shaky
i mean this in the kindest way possible—
i don't care

## I Refuse

i refuse to come from a place of weakness
that allows me to be blindsided ever again

i promise to fill myself
love myself
sustain myself
before seeking a savior

In My Cocoon

## Another Awakening

i won't say *the* awakening because time and time again it's been proven these will never be over.

but this is a radical expression of self love the death to the oblivious version of me.
i'm coming full force to claim what is owed to me.

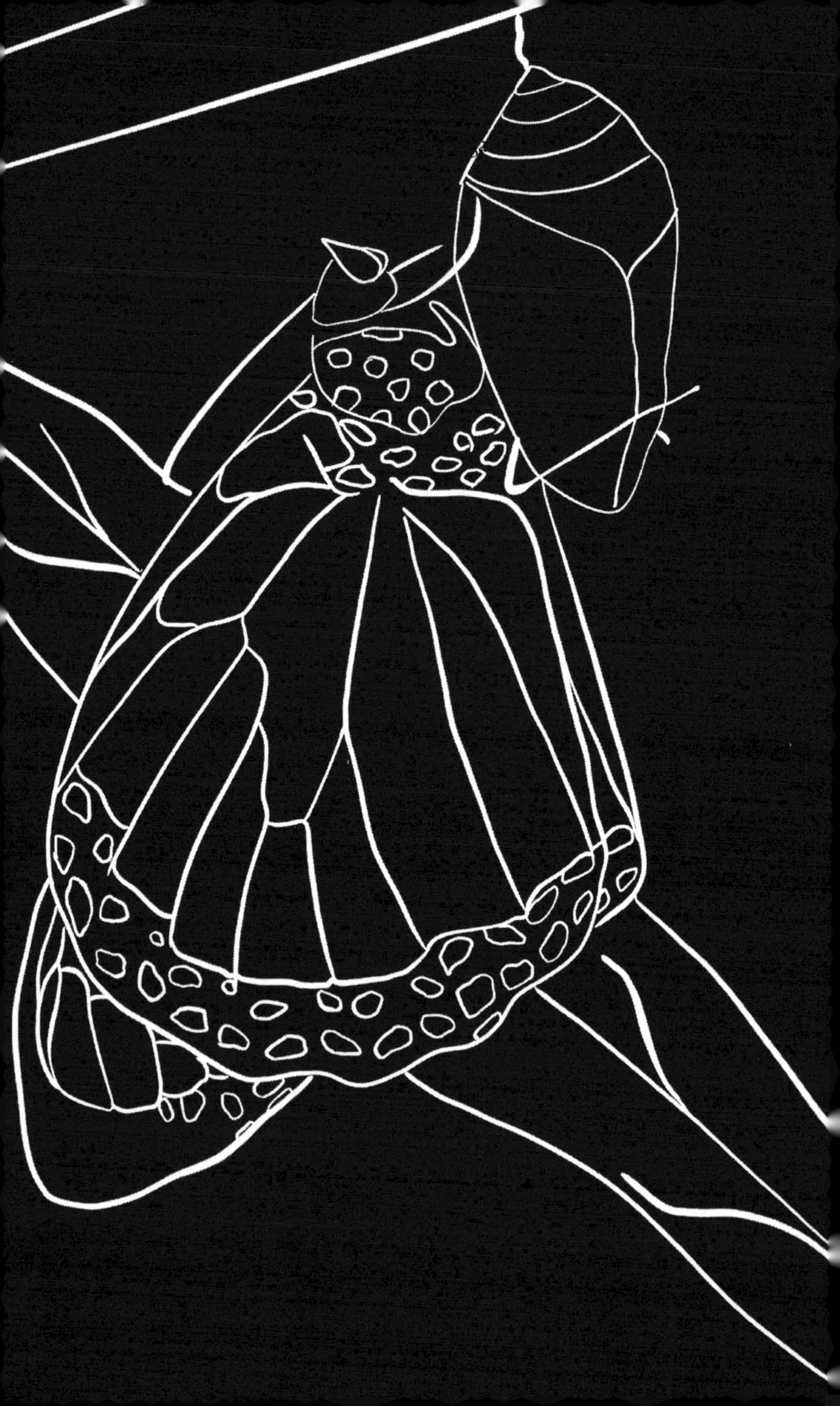

STAGE IV:
it can be so quiet
yet so loud
in this cocoon
trying to hear
my voice
above the noise

trying to remember
to surrender,
to flow

so many tempting distractions
but i am breaking free

Reyna Noriega

In My Cocoon

## Taking Risks

once i lose the flow
of being wrapped up and devoted to me
it takes too long to come back to that
and that's why i won't risk it for anybody
i used to think
i would find someone
worth the risk
but that's where i was wrong
self love comes with no exceptions
respect me as much as i respect me
raise your vibration to meet mine
or keep watching from afar

Reyna Noriega

*my lessons come in such pretty packages
maybe that's why they hurt so bad...*

In My Cocoon

and as much as i hate what you have done
to this world
i must also acknowledge what the world has
done to you
    *-for the men*

Reyna Noriega

## I'm Not Perfect

i don't know everything
i wish you could experience
the freedom i feel
admitting that out loud
i wish you could enjoy
the security of spaces
where we unveil our vulnerabilities
and accept ourselves
as we are

## In My Cocoon

fill yourself from the inside out
not the outside in
i know they world tells you
who you must be
what you must do
how you must provide
be strong
don't cry

as much as i've gone through
as a woman
i'm so glad this world
was so callous to me
because it forced me to find joy
and fulfillment within

i want the same for all of you
it is because you run on empty
you are a threat to me
and my survival

power thrills you
money drives
emotions are cast away

Reyna Noriega

## I Dream For Us All

i do this for the ones that were too focused
on surviving
too focused on pain —
to dream

In My Cocoon

## The Set Up

i think a mistake i have often made in relationships
is that i try to go swimming in shallow waters
i assume there is more beneath the surface
if only i had the magic key
and often times when the dust settles i realize
there was not much there to begin with
i retract—
it is there
but they themselves fear it and are unaware of it
i think that i can model the actions
lead them
and then cry myself to sleep at night
when i lay beside someone not able to lead me
someone more lost than i

Reyna Noriega

## Lost Together

the ones that have tried to write novels
with me as the protagonist
say that i am hard to read
while i write and plead poetically
to those that don't speak my language,
can't comprehend my truths

they aren't at that level yet
but i want them to meet me half way
not realizing when they get there
they won't know where to lead
and we will just be together,
lost

In My Cocoon

## Why Not

you're scared
and i'm tired
but because i was scared once
i will explain
what a world
that knows peace
that runs on love
looks like
do you know what community is?
no not the gated one with the guards
gatekeeping
community is love
community is peace
it is never going without
having your needs met
it is never being alone
it is working through struggle collectively
wealth has poisoned us
we kill for it
cry for it
why not destroy it

Reyna Noriega

## A Timeline

last month i was coping with heartbreak
last weekend i was crying for humanity
this week confronting systemic oppression
and sexual assault simultaneously
and now this coming weekend
i just want hugs
but they aren't allowed in a pandemic
so this load is heavy

In My Cocoon

## Exhausted

my body is exhausted
she's holding too much trauma
i'm asking my angels to hold me
spirit to guide me
i won't give up the fight
my body cannot give up on me

you will hear our cries
you erased us
silenced us
buried us
and now you will hear our cries

knowing we are in this together
gives me strength
knowing we are in this together
causes me pain

Reyna Noriega

Your feelings are not more important than
BLACK lives
Your business is not more important than
BLACK lives
Your comfort is not more important than
BLACK lives

In My Cocoon

## Drowning

you keep asking how i am
the answer is not good
because all the pain i've tried to cover
the pain inherited
from generations of trauma
the guilt of problems i cannot solve
overtakes me

Reyna Noriega

### Arms Waiting

a dream it would be
to have someone to depend on
someone to trust
to hold

i have me
i almost want to say
as if it were a radical discovery
more than enough
i love her so

but i'd still like to know
we weren't alone
in this world
that after a long day of work
there were arms waiting

In My Cocoon

## A Relief

i'm relieved
to find out you were exactly
who i thought you were
not perfect of course
no one is
but a decent human being
i told you things i've never admitted out loud to anyone
and you listened
as a friend should.
thank you.

may this be a sign
my discernment is improving

Reyna Noriega

## Lighter

now that i have revealed
and released a secret burden
i feel lighter
i can fly higher

In My Cocoon

## Wake Up

wake up, wake up, wake up
what
how
were all of our alarm clocks
set to the same time?
we're all awake,
waking up
slowly
to such a bright, bright light
it burns but i can't stop looking
my truth never louder
the secrets
everyone's secrets so naked
we're in this together
or we're not
it doesn't matter this time
because we're all awake
wake up, wake up, wake up
the world is changing
and you are new

Reyna Noriega

## Unborn

i haven't written for you in a while
sometimes i lose hope i will ever meet you
this world is so polluted,
it can be so toxic
sometimes i'm not sure
i'll ever be selfish enough
to bring you here

in my head you're safe, just a fantasy
i hold you in my heart
even if i never have you in my arms
but you came to mind today
because i remembered a promise
i made to myself
for you

i promised you i would make an impact
that greatness would be your birthright
and as i watch the revolution unfold
as i see how my art is living out its purpose
it is redefining so many narratives
it is enabling so many to imagine the unimaginable

In My Cocoon

i did it —
i don't think about that often
i just work
and i guess
i don't even know
what i work for anymore
if not for you

i'll meet you one day

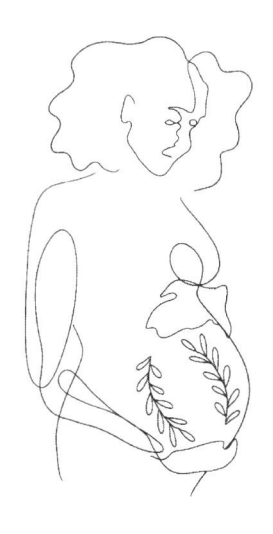

Reyna Noriega

## Letting Go

if not him then who?
the question used to scare me
make me anxious
cause me to stay too long
in the yearning
in the pleading
now when i say it
if not him then who?
i know the who
is a wish fulfilled
beyond my imagination
waiting to come in
once i let go of
him

In My Cocoon

## Timelines

you know what i think about often?
the way our timelines can be so different
as i breeze through navigating my career,
leveling up on friendships
i struggle and worry that i will never quite figure out love
i may never have the family i want to cultivate
while for others it is the opposite
in love,
parenting,
struggling to keep or create an identity apart from that
to create space for their dreams and aspirations
i hope we all figure it out
whatever our struggles are
i have manifested so much
why not this?
take time to speak gratitude onto all that has come to fruition
take time to speak gratitude for all that is still on the way

Reyna Noriega

## My Happy Place

very green
or blue
sometimes peach
where the plants are
the ocean
when the sky blushes
where the breeze kisses

## In My Cocoon

I am my best self when I am happy
I am my best self when I am whole
I am my best self when I am safe
I am my best self when I am loved
I am my best self when I am loving
I am my best self when I am supported

That is why I can't take any lukewarm lovers

Reyna Noriega

## Prepare

prepare prepare prepare
because when the blessings start coming in
when you finally remove the blocks
they come fast!

In My Cocoon

## Freedom

what does freedom look like
close your eyes
imagine with me
freedom is a clean slate
freedom is showing up as you wish
freedom is release from the chains of assumption
freedom is being able to scream, lose your temper,
make mistakes
be human
not needing to be super human
to be considered worthy of a sliver of humanity
freedom is benefit of the doubt
freedom is having your needs met
freedom is community, safety
freedom is love
and we have that
so we'll start there

Reyna Noriega

## Love Coma

i don't want to be in a comatose love state
like that feeling when you eat too much
the rest of your day becomes a blur
i need a love that invigorates me
that doesn't take center stage

In My Cocoon

## Imprint

do you know the smell of new
like the first day of school
the first night in a new home
the upper lip during a first kiss
the way that smell embeds
and imprints as a trigger
when it comes waning back
will it bring you joy
or pain

this moment smells like new
i can't wait to build memories around it

Reyna Noriega

## No Longer Asking

we were screaming for centuries
help us
love us
respect us
stripped of everything

until we stopped asking
decided to help ourselves
help each other

In My Cocoon

I want what God wants for me.

Reyna Noriega

You cannot be sad over someone who would not have given you the life that you want.
You cannot be sad over someone who cannot give you the love that you want.

In My Cocoon

**Thinking...**

i keep thinking of all the houses and dreams
i've built
with people who left
and how close i am
to having those things
for myself
it's a strange feeling
bittersweet
empowering
to want but not need

Reyna Noriega

## New Level/ New Devils

a new level
new devils
lurking
to distract
to disengage

my commitment is to me
so i will face all of these things
i will conquer them all

In My Cocoon

## No More

no more
men in transition
find yourself
grow roots
and make sure the anchor
is you
grounded
aware
open
then and only then
should you come
awaken the love inside me
when you have what it takes
to stay

Reyna Noriega

## Hold On To You

stop.
stop, just stop
stop trying to hold on to them
and please please please
hold on to you
don't loosen your grip

In My Cocoon

## **A Blessing**

when you prayed for a blessing
for an angel
for help
can't you see
it is me
everything i am
is everything you've been missing
move accordingly

Reyna Noriega

home goals:
lots of light
through the windows
and through the people
-*home*

In My Cocoon

**Welcome**

welcome conflict
welcome tension
welcome confusion

as you stir me
move through me
you force me to step up

Reyna Noriega

## Give Me

give me longevity
give me peace
give me privacy
keep the celebrity

In My Cocoon

**Let Them**

let people be honest with you
thank them for it,

even if it hurts.

Reyna Noriega

Honesty is love, accountability is love, self preservation is love.

Codependency is not.

In My Cocoon

## Be Free

allow people the freedom
to decide they don't want to be with you
whether it's in the space of friendship or romance
rejection hurts
but the other side of that
is freedom to exist
and show up fully as yourself
you are drawn to people who
barely love you
barely tolerate you
and now you are barely yourself
performing
tip-toeing
i implore you
be free

Reyna Noriega

## Forgive Yourself

without centering yourself
forgive yourself for the time
you didn't have the language
the understanding
the vocabulary

forgive yourself
so you can stop making excuses
forgive yourself
so your shame does not freeze you
and keep you from acting
from standing
forgive yourself
so that shame and fear of the unknown
does not become hate or indifference
complicity

forgive yourself, quickly
so you can join the fight
so you can stop seeking sympathy
for your ego
while people are dying
liberation is non-binary

In My Cocoon

### Tame Them

all of my wildest dreams
i tamed with discipline
and now they are reality

Reyna Noriega

## Stay Ready

this life is unpredictable
be resilient
be ready to rise
to any occasion

In My Cocoon

**her**

i'm her
i can't believe
i am her

Reyna Noriega

## For The *Soil*

my plants are a spiritual practice
in caring for them
i remember to care for myself
i remember how necessary it is to repot myself
give myself room to grow
i honor the need for light
the need for shade
time
patience

i sing to them
i sing to me

In My Cocoon

**un-*comfy***

i am so uncomfortable
what are you teaching me

i welcome it all

Reyna Noriega

Hello old friends,

It seemed impossible to grow anymore than I already had. But the universe had other plans. Isolation was a theme I touched on in In bloom. Selective isolation. Meaning I could choose when I was sick of myself and go be social. Not in the middle of a pandemic. This time, not one thing can be overlooked.

In My Cocoon

## Water You

have you considered
maybe that plant
isn't dead
beyond saving
it just needs some time in the shower
completely drenched
to fill up and perk up
please saturate yourself with love
today and everyday
whenever you need it

Reyna Noriega

## The Purge

goodbye old friend
it was really nice knowing you

goodbye old pain
you don't define me anymore

purging
letting go
so that I can ascend

In My Cocoon

## Control

i feel for the ones
that are suffering from heartache
waiting on them to change

the perpetual disappointment
of thinking you can control
you can police
how others act
or react

in my mind i see their dumbfounded faces
sad and heavy
burdened and perplexed

i can see their hands and jaws clenched
so much tension
and sadness

i wish i could show them how to let go
focus inward
leave them alone

Reyna Noriega

## Wrong Diagnosis

anything you water will grow
unless it doesn't need water…
or if it is in the wrong environment
or its roots are oversaturated
or its pot is too small

In My Cocoon

this is the revolution
and we are all the face
let that guide your decisions.

## Gratitude

I feel so whole, safe, and protected. It feels silly to ask for more.

So under this big moon I ask for nothing but I send up infinite thanks for my blessings
I am grateful that all my wishes have manifested and woven into a reality that serves my greater good.

I'm grateful that me walking in my purpose brings me peace and joy but even more so, I'm grateful I get to witness the joy it brings to others.

I'm grateful my home reflects my spirit and is a place of peace, solitude, and abundance. I pray that I continue to be like a sponge, susceptible to the lessons of the universe that allow for my growth and expansion.

I pray that I continue to move foreword with clarity of where my gifts are most needed

In My Cocoon

I pray I continue to love and welcome love
and spoil myself with the gift of acceptance
I once wanted from others.

Reyna Noriega

## All I Need

I find joy
I find peace
I find clarity in knowing
I have all I need
I am all I need

All that I want exists inside me
waiting on the right conditions to sprout
For that reason I do not yearn,
I do not envy
I just prepare.

# In My Cocoon

Let go to receive.

Reyna Noriega

There is life all around me,
I love it that way.

In My Cocoon

## Boundaries

it's so strange
the way people would like for you to
strip naked
show them all of your scars, secrets, and cards
just so they can shuffle through them
and decide they aren't interested in playing
right now

decide when you feel safe
sharing you
decide what it takes
to enter you
to experience you
know that you are worth guarding
i don't suggest you build a cave
and hide from the world
but protect yourself

Reyna Noriega

## Old You, New Pain

have you ever been fighting with someone
and in that moment you realize
you're not fighting with them at all
you are not even present
they are fighting with a past version of you

"that's not what i said"
"that's not what i meant"
it falls on deaf ears as they cite their sources

past pain
previous misunderstandings
where you didn't communicate
as best as you'd want
and now you don't understand
you're not that person anymore
your approach this time was different
it doesn't matter
that version of you in their head prevails

and in that moment you wonder
how many people
have you dwarfed in your mind

## In My Cocoon

not allowed to grow
or change or evolve
because the past pain
was enough for you
to freeze them
imprison them right there

we must learn from this
we must have more grace

Reyna Noriega

## Be Consistent

consistently learning
consistently growing
consistently working
consistently praying
consistently loving

## In My Cocoon

Black art
Black stories
Black lives
have always been valuable
           - *always*

Reyna Noriega

## Just You

i want you to not be what you are so bad
i think of how amazing it would be
if you were just
not you —
but the best thing i can do
for you
for myself
is accept that you are
just you

In My Cocoon

## Not Sustainable

it's not sustainable
the attention
you don't want the pressure
of keeping up
of staying relevant

Reyna Noriega

## Let Go To Receive

i love myself more
than my need to go back
and right any wrongs
prove myself
prove i'm worthy
they come back because they've learned
what i knew all along
i don't have to say yes
i don't have to let them
it is not rooted in a genuine opportunity
of love
of growth
of expansion
it's comfortable
it's known
but there can be beauty
in trusting that exactly what i want
exists
somewhere beyond the depths of my mind
it exists
and it is waiting with open arms
once i walk away from
the fear of it not being there

In My Cocoon

**Favors**

you are not doing me any favors
loving me thoroughly
you do yourself the favor
when you finally set your heart free

Reyna Noriega

## I Am A Magnet

when i am calm
at peace
the blessings flow in freely
there are no blocks
so why would i stress
force something
before it is my time
i am a magnet
if it doesn't come
we aren't a match

In My Cocoon

## How Many

how many more layers have to go
how many more versions do i have to know
i stand here looking at myself in the mirror
at the woman i've become
the human i've become
i like her
but i know i cannot keep her
she must continue to evolve
shed
until there is only love
and lightness
but maybe i'll get a little break
before it is time to do the work again

Reyna Noriega

## no new jails

a society that puts profit over people
is prison enough

In My Cocoon

## Sunrise Meditation

i am whole
i am filled with gratitude
i am present
i am abundant
i am wiser and more resilient than
i give myself credit for
but that changes now
i am walking in my power
believing i am deserving of the best things
therefore i am welcoming of them

Reyna Noriega

*Gratitude list:*

I am grateful for the ever changing journey and all of its beautiful surprises.

I am grateful for family and their evolving relationships.

I am grateful for growth and evolving mindsets.

I am grateful for friendships that change with the times and all the ways I show up for them and they show up for me.

I am grateful to be walking in my purpose and touching those I've intended to impact.

I am grateful I feel ready to take on new and bigger opportunities and I feel deserving of them.

I am grateful to experience new experiences with fresh but wiser eyes.

In My Cocoon

## Self Betrayal

you see how
you kept score of their sins
all those years
and not of all the times
you didn't protect you?
you didn't honor yourself
keep your promises
let's explore that

perhaps fixating on them
has allowed you
to live with yourself
a bit easier

you don't want the fragility
of hiding from your truth
face it
change it

**Routine**

Why do you stop doing
The things that work?

Reading.
Meditating.
Journaling.
Adequate sleep

Once you are in the flow
You forget
*Maintenance*

Please go back to your routine
Before you let yourself
Be thrown out of orbit

In My Cocoon

i'm at peace
i have everything i need

Reyna Noriega

## For Granted

i never thought of myself
as someone that took anything
for granted
but i never expecting
it could all stop like this
it never occurred to me
how frivolous it all was
how sacred it all was

In My Cocoon

i let everything come to me with ease.

STAGE V:
and then
a wish is fulfilled
the first sign
of light reveals
a new dawn
new life
new love
new wings

Reyna Noriega

In My Cocoon

## To Become The Butterfly

you must cocoon
shut off all the noise
cancel out all preconceived notions
of what you should be doing
and just become

Reyna Noriega

## If You Love

if you love something let it go
if you love something let it grow
if you love something let it glow

and if it comes back
with intention
with integrity
bearing gifts of love and peace

you'll know

## In My Cocoon

make sure your cocoon is a safe space.

Reyna Noriega

## Thank You For The Man

i desire so intimately
enjoy so thoroughly
and love so endlessly

i say thank you before he arrives
because i know he is on the way

In My Cocoon

## A Good Day

sometimes that perfect day
to write or to work just comes
a day that makes you stair your excuses in
the face
your to do list is clear
your energy full
the house grey because it's raining outside
at least those are perfect conditions for me
i'll turn a playlist on
that'll bring emotions to the surface
they'll help me remember all i wanted to say
and i can finally just start

Reyna Noriega

## My Love

i don't write about you
you bring me so much joy
peace
and yet
i don't think to pick up my pen
is it because the joy is so great
the peace so expansive
i have no other thought
but to enjoy you
i don't need to write
to make sense of my feelings
because you make sense
we make sense

In My Cocoon

**I Knew**

i knew i was deserving of everything i desired
and i was confident i would have everything i desired
somehow you still surprised me
somehow being held by you
still feels surreal

## Don't Fear The Cocoon

there will be times in your life
where it will necessary to be out of the mix
nurturing new relationships
projects you care deeply about
when *you* needs a bit more of *you*
don't be so consumed by the need for visibility
you rob yourself of the chance to become the butterfly

In My Cocoon

## No Rush

i am no in a rush
i let everything come to me with ease
because i know i am deserving
i am working
i am resting
i am learning gratitude
and patience
as i endure the lessons
that prepare me for the blessings

Reyna Noriega

## Grace

i give people grace
because god knows i need it too
i have watched many
who's blame and judgments
are loud and plenty
but humility and apologies
are barely audible
i don't think it is because
we forget we are flawed
but rather the awareness
makes us focus
on lack in others
to quiet our own inner critic
don't let that voice win
love others the way you want to be loved
forgive others the way you desire forgiveness
give them the space to fall
and to fail
knowing you will help them up
or at the very least,
not snicker
when they are down on the floor

In My Cocoon

## No Distractions

i will not let anyone distract me from the art —

but he is art

our life together a blank canvas

and he is not a distraction

i had no clue i was on a journey to love

but now that it's here

i am grateful for all the time i spent preparing

Reyna Noriega

## Timing

how perfect and how patient
she sits and watches
knowing —
all knowing
she gave me just enough strength
and fortitude to get me this far
and then sent you
to help complete the mission
knowing i could only do so much
go so far
alone
but that i needed to know
i was never truly alone
never in lack
so that i could appreciate you truly
cherish this more deeply
regard this more sacredly

## Full

i am full of love
i am full of patience
i am full of hope
even when it feels as though the world is closing all around me
the walls boxing me in
the pressure aiming to steal my joy
i will always find more love
more patience
more hope
endless joy

Reyna Noriega

## Higher Vibrations

i allow joy to live in me
permanently
everything that vibrates below it
must go

In My Cocoon

## My Responsibility

when i am alone
my joy
my happiness
my equilibrium
is my responsibility alone
why would i then
believe
a lover would come in
and take that responsibility from me
they may add
but never control
i must still do for me
what i have always done

Reyna Noriega

## The Quiet Ones

never underestimate the quiet ones
don't count them out just yet
they are learning
observing
planning
working
they are in their cocoon

In My Cocoon

be prepared
to shake the stem
of your best tree
to get the fruit

Reyna Noriega

## **This Time**

this time when i look in the mirror
i see my newly uncurled wings
i am stronger
i am wiser
i believe in myself more
i believe in my entitlement to joy
and to love

In My Cocoon

## Mirrors

we are mirrors
your joy my joy
your greatness my greatness
your love my love
the more abundance you feel
the more i know i can attain
there is no room for envy

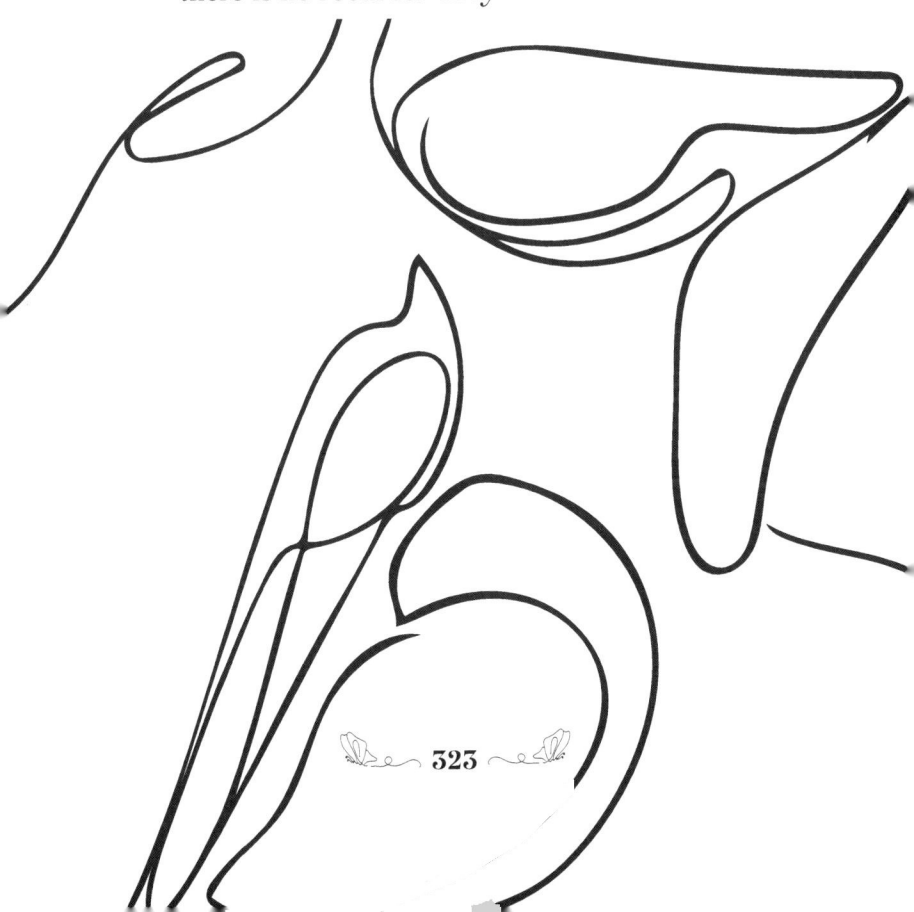

## Honey

i just want to be loved purely
ready to feel it all pour out
and over me
like warm honey
it sticks

## Love

what is love like?
well
i'm still scared
scared of losing you
scared of being disappointed by you
but also stronger in love
able to chase these fears aways

## Partnership

so this is partnership
i am pleasantly surprised
eternally grateful

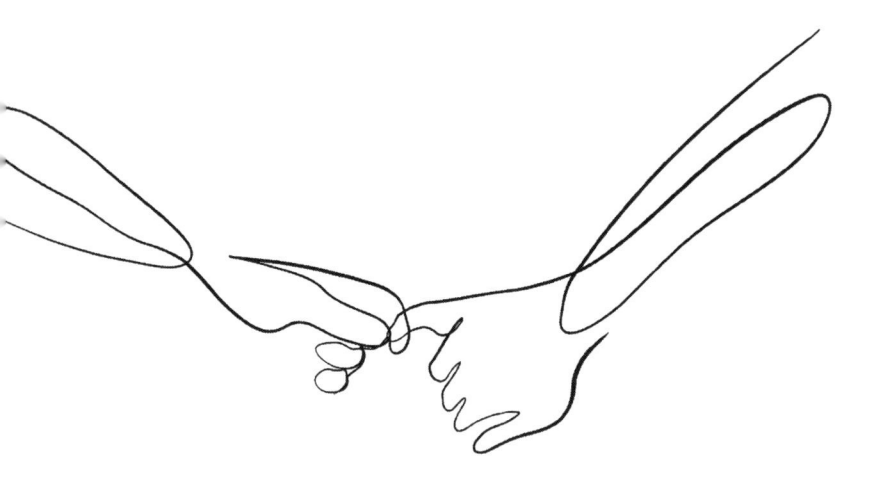

In My Cocoon

## Always More

will the luck last
will the love last
now when i ask those questions
i am not afraid
because i know the answer is yes
as long as i am true to myself
as long as i walk in my purpose
there will always be more luck
there will always be more love

Reyna Noriega

you love me the way i love me —
all love and tender consideration
you love you the way i love you —
to your core
      *-this is why it works*

In My Cocoon

## Our Palette

you've brought so much color to my life
expanded the palette with which i paint
and now i never want to go back
sharpened the lens with which i see
fortified the heart with which i love
how do i describe this feeling
all i can say is—
i am glad i was right
i am glad i healed for
i am glad i waited for
i am glad i persevered for
real love

Reyna Noriega

## Come Back

when all else fails
when you feel stuck
come back to intention
come back to your core
remember the root
remember the cause
remember the why
refine
refine
refine
reflect
could you do more
could you do better
leave comparison
leave envy
leave defeat
come back to intention
come back to you

In My Cocoon

i love being in love with you
i love you so much it ~~hurts~~
liberates

Reyna Noriega

In My Cocoon

the love scramble
i'm lost without you
i can't live without you
i'm an omelet with no egg
i love you easy
even when it's hard
your love makes me boil
you're my egg roll.
*- a poem from my love. just because it makes me smile*

Reyna Noriega

## Let Me

let me be radical proof
of what believing in yourself
can do
for you
for your dreams
for your family
for your community
so that maybe today
you start to believe
you start to trust
you stop questioning
and go

In My Cocoon

### Pleasant Surprises

this is not the journey
i thought i would be on this year
but isn't it beautiful?
i found everything i was looking for
and i didn't need to cross any borders to get it

it has made me trust my timing even more
so much i thought was lost
so little faith i had
but what is written cannot be undone

Reyna Noriega

## Suffering Twice

we end up so consumed with making sure
people don't disappoint us
we end up hurting ourselves
suffering twice
stifling experiences

show up fully
let the cards fall where they may
your boundaries are the key
honor them
and you won't have to punish yourself
or the world

## In My Cocoon

why is the awareness of love juxtaposed by
the raw, painful awareness of pain?

Reyna Noriega

## Still

still finding my voice
still suffering in silence
still holding the world on my shoulders
still weary of asking for help

In My Cocoon

## To Love Me

to love me
is to love all my waves
of deep deep emotion
of bright and airy joy
of endless inspiration

Reyna Noriega

## *Ours*

our home
our bed
our life
ours
it is all ours and i love it so

In My Cocoon

## Grief

i've never been good with words
when it comes to grief
i wish the tears i shed with you
could be enough to wrap you up
make you feel whole
wish you could see all the words i can't say
trapped and blocked within my heart
i wish any of those words would be sufficient
to make the pain go away
but they will never be
so i try to help you see
that life is meant to be lived
because it is finite
and we don't know the end
so choose love today and everyday
choose you
seek your higher self now
now is the time for change
now is the time for more
now is the time for greater
if not for you
do it for all those that won't see tomorrow
do it for the ones we have lost

Reyna Noriega

## Thinking Of Oppression

Lately, my mind has been in a loop. Trying to understand what i feel, trying to find a solution to all the worlds ailments. Throughout that process, I hide a very important part of myself from the person I love most. He knows me to be strong, witty, humorous, but what will he think of the girl that looses sleep over the pain of the lack of solutions. The girl who cries for the whole world, and myself all at once.
I guess the thoughts and feelings have been building for some time. Usually a feeling bothers me until I take the time to face it, dissect it, and understand it.

## In My Cocoon

I create to forget. I create to offer smiles, because this life steals so many.
I weep for the murdered and i weep for the murderer created by circumstance of those that do not understand love. I have long ago found the common thread of evil— power. I believe people find the same ecstasy in power that they would find in love if they did not fear it so.

Violence begets violence.
Our nation was built on violence and we see it manifest over and over and over.

We are defined by greed and consolidation of power and goods. The gap between those who have resources and power widens daily. So why not turn away from it? Say no to the whole system? Instead of choosing love and building our communities on that foundation, we find more and more ways to separate ourselves and create barriers.

Whether religious, political, or otherwise,

people join groups to feel connected and to have a sense of community. Why do people often times take away a key component of community? They strip these communities of true love and care and what we are left with is gatekeeping and extremism.

"Never forget that justice is what love looks like in public." -Cornel west
I would love to see more justice, i would love to see more love.

In My Cocoon

***all that you are...***

i sit and marvel
at the way you are
the literal manifestation
of all i have imagined
someone to laugh with,
someone to love,
someone to share with —
moments, projects, ideas, dreams.
someone to look forward with
into an uncertain future
and feel safe

***...all that i need***

Reyna Noriega

i am
replacing feelings of anxiety with gratitude
and bravery
- *a mantra*

In My Cocoon

## I Deserve

i deserve
safety
protection
love i don't have to question
trust
honesty
i deserve love

we've made such a mess of that word
piecing together context clues haphazardly
no wonder we pass off possession
and entitlement
dishonesty and disloyalty
as love

no wonder we need contracts to tell us
what our hearts should intuitively know
and you may not know yet
but i hope you learn soon
that you deserve,
the same way i deserve,
a love that is true

Reyna Noriega

*i love you*

my heart beats in
i love you's
and when it overflows
they escape my lips

In My Cocoon

## Change

what will i have to sacrifice next
to remain great
will it be rest?
that's non-negotiable
with it be the friendships
i so carefully nurtured
no —
but as i feel myself expand
i feel like my limbs are being pulled in so many directions
i can't remain who i was
solely out of the fear they'll say
"you've changed"
change i must

Reyna Noriega

## Can You Feel It?

can you feel my love for you
i wonder if you feel the pulse in my fingertips
as i caress you
as i take care to run them along your back
i feel the pulse
the electricity —
it moves through me
does it move through you?

In My Cocoon

living for me*

　　*and whoever loves and respects me
enough to stay.

Reyna Noriega

## Remembering

i've been taking a trip down memory lane
the photos bring back memories
so much gratitude fills me
as i realize
i've lived a full life
full of love
full of laughter
free of fear

In My Cocoon

## Keep Looking

people never lose their air of mystery
sometimes we forget to look
we take what we know
how much we know
for granted
not realizing there are waves
and depths
and changes
we won't see
if we stop looking

Reyna Noriega

## Moments

sometimes the sum
of all of my experiences
creeps up on me
all of a sudden
i am the sum of views and smells
i've momentarily forgotten
moments treasured
moments stolen
dreams realized
some forgotten
kisses
tears
anger
realizations
i realize in those moments
how rich i truly am

In My Cocoon

you are your first home
take care of you.

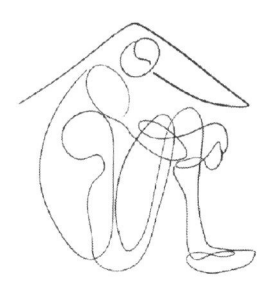

355

Reyna Noriega

we speak so politely
like strangers
i long to know you
i wonder at what moment i stopped knowing you
was it when we stopped sharing rooms?
when we no longer had the opportunity to talk ourselves to sleep?
did we grow and morph and mature on separate tangents?
was it college? did it change you?
did i change in your absence?
was my transformation unrecognizable?
did i utter a criticism carelessly that made you feel judged or unloved by me?
or was the poison something beyond our control, something we inherited?

*-some relationships still need mending*

In My Cocoon

## Change. Or Don't.

it is true.
you do not have to change to please anyone
but if that is rooted upon selfishness and a
blatant disregard for others feelings,
please do not be surprised when they change
to protect themselves from you

Reyna Noriega

## Life With You

living life with you
is the dream i never dared to dream
and it is better than i could've imagined

In My Cocoon

*"the world is still burning  
but [life with you] is a vacation"*

Reyna Noriega

## Thinking Of Next

i've done a lot
created so much magic
and for many it would satisfy
but even now
i can feel my bones itch
as they feel too big for this current body
i will shed again
i will grow again
i will evolve once more
i know that much is true
where will we go?
who will we touch?
when will i meet you?

In My Cocoon

## Let It Be

how funny
that when i finally allow you
to be who you want to be
when i stop trying to control
mold
predict
you would be exactly who i needed you to
be

Reyna Noriega

## The Pinch

why are you so afraid to meet yourself
what are you so afraid to find
i promise the pinch only lasts a moment
the realization that it has been you
and only you
that has held you back all along

but that pinch is what it takes
to finally get your wings

In My Cocoon

## Prepare

whatever you are praying for
whatever you are dreaming of
prepare prepare prepare
until it is yours
there's nothing worse
than a blessing that slips
through our fingers

Reyna Noriega

## **Please Rest**

it is in my calm,
it is in my rest
that i see things the most clear
it is there my best ideas are born
out of flow
rather than desperation
please rest

In My Cocoon

## Like Water

my love
i love waking up to you
you are every answered prayer
i can see the homes i'm building with you
both physical and figurative
like water we flow
together
the same direction
yet unrestrained

Reyna Noriega

## In My Cocoon

in my cocoon of feelings and introspection
i was able to make sense of who i wanted to be
i was able to make sense of
how i was meant to serve
and show up in that body and in that mindset
confidently

it was birthed from uncertainty
anxiety
and a sea of fear
but eventually i gave up
i gave in
and surrendered once again to the moment
and what it was bringing and teaching

all of my titles are frivolous
what i am
at my core
is a vessel
a translator

the universe speaks

## In My Cocoon

i listen
i live it
so that you may watch
and you may learn
and we can perhaps, save this dying world
together
with love

Reyna Noriega

## I Am Art

i belong in beautiful dresses
beautiful gowns
i am as much
a work of art
as any of my canvases
i know that now
i own that now

In My Cocoon

## Mind Games

our minds play crazy tricks on us
because it's never been done before
we believe it is impossible
and if it is being done
we believe there will be no room for us

Reyna Noriega

**Things I've learned:**

Be a student
Be a sponge
Learn and observe
Learn and absorb
Squeeze
Rinse
Repeat

In My Cocoon

## As A Mama

The gift I want to give my daughter
Is acceptance
I know all too well the dynamic
I will decline the chance to be her fiercest critic
To pick at her scabs
Because I know that the world
Will do enough of that on its own
Is that why
It is easier for mother's and sons
Why they get along
Because in them they see reflected
The favor of the world
And in daughters they see the pain
The judgment
The condemnation
So generation after generation
Mother's have elected to prepare their daughters for war
And prepare their sons for favor Believe in magic
Whatever you do
Believe believe believe

## Family

go easy on each other
remember it is both a gift
and curse
to know someone so intimately
to know a bad side
or a real side
the side with no mirrors

In My Cocoon

Look at everything we were able to build
by centering love.

Reyna Noriega

## How Many

How many moments
Have I robbed myself of
Disconnected
From God
From Source
From Gratitude
Plugged into
Worry
Doubt
Unrest

In My Cocoon

**And Now**

the dream now
is not searching
or being
or doing

the dream now is peace
and rest
and attracting

Reyna Noriega

## Still Learning

Being in love is teaching me, that I still have work to do.
All this love in my heart and I can still be self centered.
I can still be egotistical.
I can still be the wounded child.
I can wrongfully take those wounds out on my partner.
I can avoid the work with love.

I am aware of these things now.
I can work on these things now.
I can prevent the strain I once felt was inevitable.
I can communicate better.
I can express myself better.

It doesn't make me feel less than to know this.
It makes me feel in charge of my fate, *our fate*.

## In My Cocoon

Being intentional of what I take in,
So I can be in control of what I put out.

Reyna Noriega

## Follow The Magic

Follow the magic
Search if it's not around
Create it if you need

In My Cocoon

**Elevate, Evolve, Flow**

i elevate
to ensure i stay
as close to Gods plan
as possible

Reyna Noriega

shed the skin
that convinces you
a full life
a full love
is not your birthright

In My Cocoon

Thank you,
For the gift of making me feel easy to love.
Doing the work to understand my patterns
and give me the benefit of the doubt.

I looking forward to being able to
reciprocate that gift as we grow.

There's work I still need to do internally to
control self sabotaging thoughts but I feel
lucky that I can follow your example.

It makes the work easier, when the love
just flows.

*you deserve...*

# About the
# AUTHOR

*Get in touch*
*hello@ reynanoriega.com*
📷 *@ reynanoriega*
🐦 *@ reynasnoriega*

PHOTO CREDIT: NICHOLAS FIGARO

## About The Author

*Reyna Noriega* is a 28 year old Visual Artist and Author born, raised, and working in Miami, FL. Having seen the power of introspection, self reflection, and healing, Reyna's work centers that aspect of our journey as we seek to rise and be our best, most authentic selves so that people may experience sustainable peace and happiness.

In her creative work, she has centered women of color. As an Afro-Caribbean Latina, she has seen firsthand how damaging it can be when you don't see positive representation of yourself. She aims to fill the world with vibrant, joyful depictions of marginalized peoples. Her work has graced the cover of Science Magazine and The New Yorker and thousands of people collect and showcase her art in their homes around the world.

Her writings are muses from her own journey condensed into a poetic form that people can digest and insert their own experiences, similar to her faceless drawings. She aims not to be a voice for the voiceless, but to lead them to their own voice.

Reyna Noriega

# For Reflecting

In My Cocoon

# For Dreaming

Made in the USA
Columbia, SC
02 April 2022